The 500 Hidden Secrets of

THE HAGUE

INTRODUCTION

There are many reasons why you should plan a visit to The Hague.
It's the city where the government has its seats and the Dutch royal
family resides of course, but it's also the international city of peace and
justice, the only large Dutch city by the sea, one of the greenest cities
of the Netherlands, and it can boast a long and rich history. This guide
takes you off the beaten path and leads you to the most interesting
and often unknown places in The Hague. Looking for the most
impressive views of the coastline and the skyline? Do you like chilling
in beautiful secret gardens and century-old courtyards? Do you enjoy
an outstanding Indonesian meal or a succulent Dutch herring? Or do
you want to learn how to make your own Dutch wine? This and much
more is what you'll discover in this book.

Because of its many international organisations, thousands of expats
settle in The Hague. If you happen to be one of them, this guide is
perfect for you: it will help you to navigate the city and to get to know
it from a different (non-tourist) perspective. This guide encourages
you to look further than the usual hotspots. Walk to the far end of the
beach to find peace and quiet, try a beer from a hidden monastery,
discover cutting-edge art in a former power plant. Of the highlights
included, lesser-known aspects are revealed. For example, when you're
at the Mauritshuis, this guide will lead you to the modern ceiling
mural, or to the garden of the Peace Palace.

This book is an intimate guide to the places the author would
recommend to friends who want to discover the real The Hague.

HOW TO
USE THIS BOOK?

———————

This book lists 500 things you need to know about The Hague in 100 different categories. Most of these are places to visit, with practical information to help you find your way. Others are bits of information that help you get to know the city and its habitants. The aim of this guide is to inspire, not to cover the city from A to Z.

The places listed in the guide are given an address, including the neighbourhood and a number. The neighbourhood and number allow you to find the locations on the maps at the beginning of the book: first look for the map of the corresponding neighbourhood, then look for the right number. A word of caution however: these maps are not detailed enough to allow you to find specific locations in the city. You can obtain an excellent map from any tourist office or in most hotels, or you can locate the addresses on your smartphone.

Please also bear in mind that cities change all the time. The chef who hits a high note one day may be uninspiring on the day you happen to visit. The hotel ecstatically reviewed in this book might suddenly go downhill under a new manager. Or the bar recommended as one of 'the 5 best bars to drink with the locals' might be empty on the night you visit. This is obviously a highly personal selection. You might not always agree with it. If you want to leave a comment, recommend a bar or reveal your favourite secret place, please visit the website *the500hiddensecrets.com* or follow *@500hiddensecrets* on Instagram or Facebook and leave a comment.

THE AUTHOR

Tal Maes moved to The Hague in her early twenties and immediately fell in love with this royal and green city by the sea. As a city girl who loves to explore nature, Tal finds The Hague the perfect city in the Netherlands to live in: it offers the creative energy and impulses that come with city life, but at the same time you'll be amazed by the stunning bits of nature in and around the city, like beaches, parks, forests and even lakes.

Tal loves to spend time outdoors: biking, hiking, picnicking or enjoying a peaceful boat trip. But as a photographer and food and travel writer, she is also all about exploring the urban life in her hometown. Museums, cultural events, festivals, restaurants, bars, shops: Tal somehow knows about every event or new place that opens. So when you're in The Hague, you might spot Tal on her bike and with her camera at hand, crossing the entire city to discover what's new and hot and what's hidden and rare.

Tal has written about and photographed her city before, so listing and describing her 500 favourite places in The Hague was right up her alley. However, she couldn't have done it without the help of her always devoted husband HP, who is just as eager to discover everything what The Hague has to offer as she is. Nor could she have completed this guide without the insider tips of locals, friends and entrepreneurs. She is grateful for everyone's precious help.

THE HAGUE

overview

North Sea

3 + 5
Scheveningen

6
Haagse Hout

8
Segbroek

1 + 2 + 4
Centre

7
Voorburg

7
Laak

9
Loosduinen

7
Leidschenveen-
Ypenburg

9
Escamp

Map 1
CENTRE
OLD CENTRE, CHINATOWN
and STATIONSBUURT

Map 2
CENTRE
HOFKWARTIER and VOORHOUT

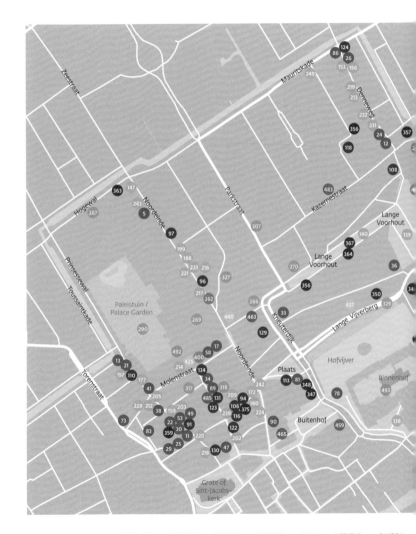

UILEBOMEN *and* STATIONSBUURT

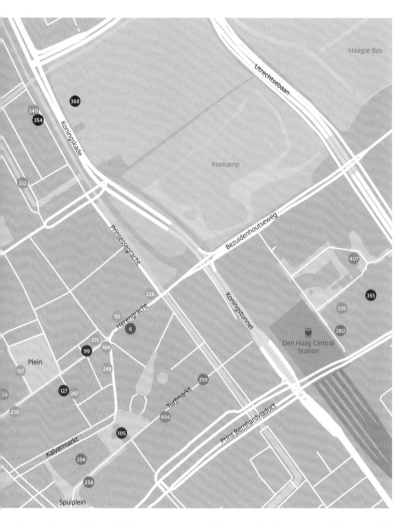

Map 3
SCHEVENINGEN
STATENKWARTIER, ZORGVLIET
and DUINOORD

EAT — DRINK — SHOP — BUILDINGS — DISCOVER — CULTURE — CHILDREN — SLEEP — WEEKEND — RANDOM

Map 4

CENTRE

ARCHIPEL, WILLEMSPARK
and ZEEHELDENKWARTIER

Cemetery
Kerkhoflaan
325

Cemetery
St. Petrus Banden
324

62

208

Oostduin

Riouwstraat

60

145
149 423

Raamweg

Raamweg

321

Jewish
Cemetery

Burgemeester Patijnlaan

Burgemeester
de Monchypark

298

276

330

37

314
314

1 132

211

193

16

Javastraat

Koningskade

Wassenaarseweg

424

222 223

210

374

Zuid Holland-
plein

Vredespaleis /
Peace Palace

137 281

194

107

408

422 112

Laan van Meerdervoort

436

344

443 480

Zeestraat

Mauritskade

Koningskade

92
18
196
197
173
183 85
195 2 190

398

234
335

Hogewal

Noordeinde

Parkstraat

Lange Voorhout

Lange
Voorhout

14

241

23 121

Paleistuin /
Palace Garden

Hofvijver

Map 5

SCHEVENINGEN

WESTDUINPARK, HARBOUR,
BEACH, OLD TOWN *and* VISSERIJBUURT

BELGISCH PARK, WESTBROEKPARK
and SCHEVENINGSE BOSJES

Oostduinpark

Oostduinen

Zwolsestraat

Harstenhoekweg

184

Stevinstraat

303

244

Doorniksestraat

Van Alkemadelaan

Nieuwe Parklaan

114

305

353

100

Pompstationsweg

282

Nieuwe
Scheveningse
Bosjes

Westbroekpark

334   420 287 369

Haringkade

Hubertustunnel

265

St. Hubertus-
park

315

Ruychrocklaan

304

Professor B.M. Teldersweg

Plesmanweg

296

288

Scheveningse
Bosjes

Cemetery
Kerkhoflaan

Raamweg

Oostduinlaan

Oostduin

Scheveningseweg

Cemetery
St. Petrus Banden

392

Map 6

HAAGSE HOUT

and SUBURBS NORTH

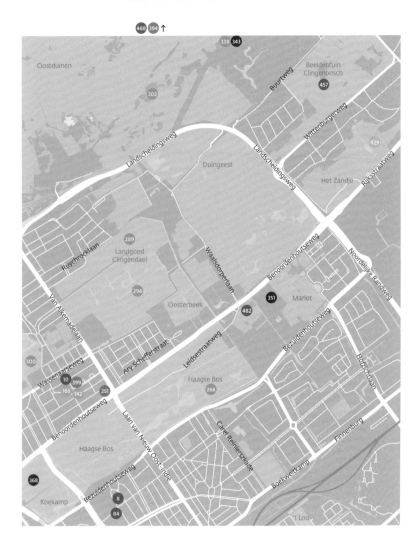

Map 7

EAST

LAAK, VOORBURG and
LEIDSCHENVEEN-YPENBURG

EAT — **DRINK** — SHOP — BUILDINGS — DISCOVER — **CULTURE** — CHILDREN — SLEEP — **WEEKEND** — RANDOM

Map 8
SEGBROEK

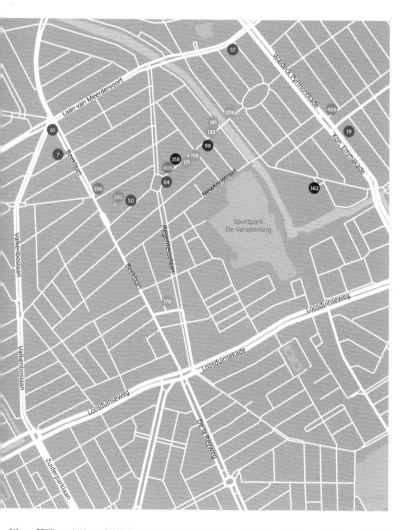

Map 9
SOUTH
LOOSDUINEN *and* SUBURBS SOUTH

North Sea

415
469
253

427

Park Meer
en Bos

389
Kijkduin

448

Park
Ockenburgh

De Zandmotor

467

416 470

32

Westduinen

419
320

Monsterseweg

Madestein

451

Haagweg

Nieuweweg

48

Madeweg

Poeldijkseweg

475

Zwartendijk

Kon. Julianaweg

Het Prinsen-
bos

473

ESCAMP, SCHILDERSWIJK
and SUBURBS SOUTH

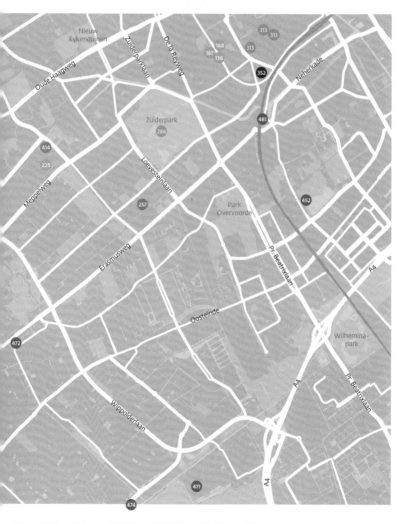

LORELEI

90 PLACES TO
EAT GOOD FOOD

The 5 best places for **BREAKFAST & BRUNCH** —— 24

5 of the city's best places for **LUNCH** —————— 27

5 places where you can enjoy **HEALTHY FOOD** —— 29

The 5 best restaurants for
VEGETARIAN and **VEGAN** food ——————— 31

5 cosy places for **EXCEPTIONAL COOKING** —— 33

5 great restaurants with a **MODERN CUISINE** —— 35

5 restaurants with **AN IMPRESSIVE DECOR** —— 37

The 5 best places to eat **FRESH FISH** ————— 40

The 5 best spots for **INDONESIAN FOOD** ——— 42

5 casual places to enjoy **ASIAN CUISINE** ——— 44

5 great **CHINESE RESTAURANTS** ————— 46

5 relaxed places for good ITALIAN FOOD ——— 48

The 5 best NEIGHBOURHOOD
RESTAURANTS ——————————————— 50

The 5 best places to EAT AT THE BEACH ——— 52

The 5 best spots for A QUICK BITE —————— 54

The 5 best places to enjoy DUTCH HERRING —— 56

5 excellent ICE-CREAM SHOPS —————— 58

5 LOCAL SPECIALITIES you must try ——— 60

The 5 best places for
BREAKFAST & BRUNCH

---

1 **PEPPERMINT**
Frederikstraat 983
Willemspark ④
+31 (0)70 365 91 82

Peppermint hasn't changed much since its opening in 1973, nor has its menu. No hip overnight oats or açai bowls here, but good old-fashioned scrambled eggs or *uitsmijters* (a slice of bread with fried eggs and ham or cheese) instead. The Dutch celebrity chef Yvette van Boven worked here before she became famous. She painted several recipes on the wall in her characteristic handwriting.

2 **CRUNCH**
Piet Heinstraat 108-A
Zeeheldenkwartier ④
+31 (0)70 364 05 52
crunchcafe.nl

This cute cafe was one of the first hip places for coffee and breakfast in The Hague. On weekends, it can be packed with people in need for a good coffee and a *Full English Breakfast* with all the extras, like sausages and baked beans. Crunch also offers other alluring dishes, like pancakes, French toast and bagels.

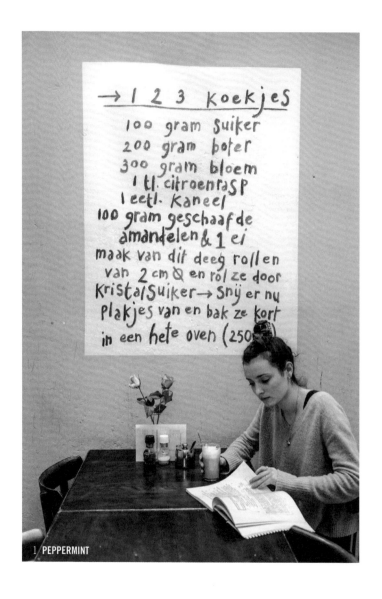

→ 1 2 3 koekjes
100 gram suiker
200 gram boter
300 gram bloem
1 tl. citroenrasp
1 eetl. kaneel
100 gram geschaafde
amandelen & 1 ei
maak van dit deeg rollen
van 2 cm Ø en rol ze door
kristalsuiker → snij er nu
plakjes van en bak ze kort
in een hete oven (250°)

1 / PEPPERMINT

3 DE OVERKANT

Stationsweg 32
Stationsbuurt ①
+31 (0)70 445 14 80
naardeoverkant.nl

De Overkant is a favourite among locals for breakfast, coffee and lunch. This very informal place opens at 8 am and is perfect for an early morning coffee with a croissant or a sandwich with a freshly pressed juice. In summer, enjoy breakfast or a piece of homemade pie on the lush terrace in the city park.

4 CLUB VERS

Stationsweg 136-A
Stationsbuurt ①
+31 (0)70 891 28 60
clubvers.nl

This trendy day-time restaurant pleases everyone: vegetarians, vegans, meat eaters and kids. The focus lies on healthy as the kitchen likes to work with fresh veggies and fruits. Start a lazy Sunday here with a healthy pitaya smoothie bowl or pancakes with homemade hazelnut-chocolate spread and strawberries.

5 SAM SAM

Noordeinde 162
Hofkwartier ②
+31 (0)70 406 10 57
samsamdenhaag.nl

You can put together your own healthy menu at this hip and modern cafe for breakfast and lunch. Choose a base like an açai bowl, a green bowl, or yoghurt; add some fruit, grains and seeds or nuts. Sam Sam also serves eggs on toast and on top, for example, avocado, spinach and salmon.

5 of the city's best places for
LUNCH

6 **BARTINE**

Herengracht 11-A
Old Centre ②
+31 (0)70 204 24 44
bartine.co

In the heart of the shopping area, Bartine is a great place for lunch. The Middle Eastern dishes are an explosion of flavours and a feast for the eye. Do not expect the average avocado sandwich here, but invented dishes such as burrata with caramelised fennel and burnt leek.

6 BARTINE

7 POMPERNIKKEL

Beeklaan 370
Segbroek ⑧
+31 (0)70 737 00 44
pompernikkel.nl

The owner is very passionate about homemade organic breads, patisserie, pizza and top-quality products. The result is a hip neighbourhood place where you order at the counter and can have lunch inside or outside. Also open for breakfast and coffee. We love this place!

8 BAARDMAN

Theresiastraat 18-A
Haagse Hout ⑥
+31 (0)70 406 65 59
*restaurant
baardman.nl*

This street might not be the most romantic street of The Hague, but lunch (or dinner!) at Baardman certainly makes up for it. At this cool restaurant with minimalist design and old ornamental plaster ceilings they serve modern Mediterranean food. Think inventive sandwiches, some fabulous egg dishes *(tortilla de bacalao* with glazed onions), as well as salads.

9 HAVER

Reinkenstraat 103
Scheveningen –
Duinoord ③
+31 (0)70 213 63 99
proefhaver.nl

Since its opening, this hip neighbourhood cafe has been a hit with locals. The lunch menu contains many healthy options, homemade and fresh, loaded with veggies. Haver also serves superb vegetarian and vegan sandwiches, like the one with avocado, mango, mint and a pepper-cashew spread.

10 LE PETIT QUARTIER

Van Hoytema-
straat 96
Haagse Hout ⑥
+31 (0)70 800 21 22
www.petit-quartier.nl

This somewhat quiet neighbourhood really needed a relaxed place like Le Petit Quartier. A lively place where you can bring your kids or where you can meet friends for lunch. On the menu are many sandwiches (the *baguettes*), as well as salads and a homemade soup of the day.

5 places where you can enjoy
HEALTHY FOOD

---

11 OHANA POKÉ AND MORE

Prinsestraat 18
Hofkwartier ②
+31 (0)70 737 05 80
ohanapoke.nl

The Hawaiian *poké* has conquered the foodie world. Not surprisingly so, for it's a delicious healthy treat. At Ohana Poké you can either have a bowl or a *sushirrito*, a sushi burrito stuffed with rice, veggies, shrimp, tuna, tofu or chicken. Eat your healthy lunch or early dinner at one of the few tables in this canteen-like restaurant.

12 SAPLAB SLOWJUICE

Denneweg 8
Voorhout ②
+31 (0)6 25 35 03 02
saplab.nl

The Hague is on a roll with young and fresh entrepreneurs! Two sisters, Elise and Caroline, opened a cool little slow juice bar in the heart of the city on Denneweg. They make wonderful juices, smoothies, boosters, and healthy bowls and snacks. Drinks and food that make you feel good and brighten up your day.

13 PISTACHE CAFÉ

Prinsestraat 134
Hofkwartier ②
+31 (0)70 362 62 10
pistachecafe.nl

This pretty cafe on the corner of one of the liveliest streets in town serves modern healthy sandwiches, salads, panini, smoothies and freshly pressed juices. You can even order a well-stocked picnic basket to take with you into the greens of the Palace Garden just across the street.

14 BUDDHA BOWL

Prins Hendrik-
plein 22
Zeeheldenkwartier ④
+31 (0)70 225 16 10
buddhabowl-
denhaag.nl

Find your inner calm and zen with a slow juice, smoothie bowl, Holi Moli Dal soup, or Buddha bowl. This laid-back health food spot is a perfect fit for this neighbourhood where many young professionals live. Next to a popular yoga studio, this is also the place where many yogis begin (or end) a yoga class.

15 JUNI CAFÉ

AT: HET NUTSHUIS
Riviervismarkt 5
Old Centre ①
+31 (0)70 820 07 94
junilekkernijen.nl

Maybe this is the most hidden cafe of The Hague. Located in the Nutshuis, a former bank, and overlooking the ecological Nutsgarden, it's the perfect spot to enjoy a healthy breakfast or lunch. Assemble a plate with vegetarian food at the salad bar or order organic sandwiches straight from the menu. Juni's homemade cakes are a real treat, too.

15 JUNI CAFÉ

The 5 best restaurants for
VEGETARIAN and
VEGAN food

16 FOAM

Frederikstraat 44
Willemspark ④
+31 (0)70 752 21 41
foam-den-haag.nl

With inventive dishes such as spicy *quesadillas* stuffed with bean cheese, a grilled cheese sandwich with cashew cream cheese, or scrumptious pancakes with salted caramel sauce, you can even bring your meat-eating friends to this day-time restaurant. In summer, you can enjoy lunch in the cute little garden. A must-visit.

17 VEGAN PIZZA BAR

Molenstraat 15
Hofkwartier ②
+31 (0)6 43 61 03 18
veganpizzabar.com

We love the motto of this urban pizza bar: 'Eating vegan is not hard'. Once you've tasted their pizza, lasagna and sides, you'll agree. The secret is the surprisingly good homemade vegan cheese, which is used as topping on the pizza and lasagne. Check out their pizzas with funky names.

18 PLENTY

Piet Heinstraat 37
Zeeheldenkwartier ④
+31 (0)6 51 08 38 04
plentydenhaag.nl

With the plant-based revolution that's going on, this beautiful vegan daytime restaurant is a hit. The owners really master the art of vegan cooking. Out of their open kitchen come delicious breakfast and lunch dishes, like flower granola and roasted cauliflower with *muhammara*.

19 HAGEDIS

**Waldeck Pyrmont-
kade 116
Zeehelden-
kwartier** ③⑧
+31 (0)70 364 04 56
restauranthagedis.nl

This beautifully tiled restaurant is situated in the former entrance hall of an old school building. Since its opening in 2004, Hagedis has been famous for its cheese fondue. Since the restaurant turned vegan, you can order 'cashew cheese' fondue. If you are not into fondue at all: there are many other vegan dishes to choose from.

20 HUMMUS

**Prins Hendrik-
straat 60
Zeeheldenkwartier** ③
+31 (0)70 888 15 46
ilovehummus.nl

At this bright modern place, they serve Mediterranean and Middle Eastern soul food, such as *shakshuka*, falafel, roasted aubergine and fried cauliflower. But also inventive dishes like a 'pink devil burger', a pink bun with a veggie *kofte* burger and mango mayonnaise. Their velvety hummus comes with various toppings and is served with homemade pita bread and a refreshing coleslaw.

20 HUMMUS

5 cosy places for
EXCEPTIONAL COOKING

---

21 BØG

Prinsestraat 130
Hofkwartier ②
+31 (0)70 406 90 44
bøg.com

Food lovers should eat at this chic yet intimate Danish restaurant with a 'new Nordic cuisine'. A restaurant where everything is well balanced and pure in a Scandinavian way: from the beautiful sober wooden interior to the exquisite stunningly presented food. Bøg serves a non-vegetarian and a vegetarian six-course menu, made with organic ingredients.

22 PORTFOLIO

Prinsestraat 36
Hofkwartier ②
+31 (0)70 219 96 91
portfolio-restaurant.nl

This modern little restaurant attracts local foodies of all ages. Out of the open kitchen comes a regularly alternating chef's menu with nine small delicate dishes. You can either sit at the counter and get a glimpse of what the chefs prepare, or settle down at one of the few tables. Its natural wines are a real treat, too.

23 TOMMY'S & ZUURVEEN

Veenkade 19
Zeeheldenkwartier ④
+31 (0)71 753 22 74
tommysenzuurveen.nl

Fine dining in a casual setting. The Hague is fortunate to have Tommy's & Zuurveen, where chef Teun Zuurveen (who also worked for Michelin-star chefs Niven Kunz and Jonnie Boer) and owner-host Tom Janssen create the most wonderful dishes and ambiance. You can choose between two three-course menus, one with meat and fish and one vegetarian.

24 OOGST

Denneweg 10-B
Voorhout ②
+31 (0)70 360 92 24
restaurantoogst.nl

If Michelin-star restaurants are not for your budget, but you want to enjoy the same quality food, go to restaurant Oogst. It shares the owner and the produce from the nearby organic vegetable garden with one-star restaurant Calla's. The prices of the menus are very decent, considering the quality of the food and wine.

25 RESTAURANT 6&24

Nobelstraat 13
Hofkwartier ②
+31 (0)70 219 68 48
restaurant6en24.nl

The owners, Rik van de Laar and Saskia de Kuijer, met and gained experience at no place less than the three-Michelin-star restaurant De Librije. Now they run a trendy yet elegant restaurant in downtown The Hague. Rik is the creative chef, while Saskia takes care of the wine. High-quality food in a modern and inviting environment.

5 great restaurants with a
MODERN CUISINE

26 **WALTER BENEDICT**
Denneweg 69-A
Voorhout ②
+31 (0)70 785 37 45
walterbenedict.nl

From early morning till late at night, this cafe-bistro is crowded and vibrant. Local residents have breakfast, lunch and dinner here, or they meet after work for a perfect gin-tonic or a speciality beer with charcuterie or oysters. Expect modern bistro dishes with seasonal ingredients, like sautéed wild scallops, steak tartare, sautéed mussels and grilled chicken Provençal.

27 **GLASWERK**
Fokkerkade 14
Laak ⑦
+31 (0)70 214 91 64
glaswerkdenhaag.nl

The location of this restaurant, on the waterfront in the industrial Binckhorst, is quite rough. Yet the cuisine of this urban restaurant is refined, light and modern with a changing menu. In summer the lovely terrace is the place you want to be! You can even come by boat and moor in the little harbour.

28 ZEBEDEÜS

Rond de Grote Kerk 8
Old Centre ①
+31 (0)70 346 83 93
zebedeus.nl

Despite its centuries-old premises in the Great or St James' Church, the restaurant has a modern look and vibe. Ever since its opening 20 years ago, it has worked with local and organic produce and hip ingredients. On sunny days, the beautiful terrace under old sycamores is a great place for lunch.

29 RESTAURANT Ñ

Nobelstraat 22
Hofkwartier ②
+31 (0)70 444 33 03
restaurant-n.nl

As if you've landed on a Mediterranean square! This little informal restaurant serves exquisite modern Spanish dishes to share. Grilled *pulpo* with sunchokes, grilled razor clams with vinaigrette *anisado*, steak *a la plancha* with *champiñones al ajillo*. The vibes are totally relaxed and in summer the terrace is one of the most romantic places to eat outside.

30 QUERU CANTINA MEXICANA

Prinsestraat 30
Hofkwartier ②
+31 (0)70 331 10 51
cantinaqueru.com

At this Mexican *cantina* you'll get Mexican dishes with a modern twist. The menu is small but inviting. Tacos with succulent flank steak with black garlic and orange, tortillas with refried beans, poached eggs, cactus and salsa verde. Everything is beautifully presented. Do not forget to order one of the excellent cocktails!

5 restaurants with
AN IMPRESSIVE DECOR

---

31 LITTLE V
Rabbijn Maarsen-
plein 21
Chinatown ①
+31 (0)70 392 12 30
littlev.nl

Inside this large Vietnamese restaurant, it feels like you are in the tropics. This lively place with a lot of wood, bamboo and plants has the perfect ambiance for the Vietnamese street food they serve: mostly small plates, mildly spiced and with lots of the characteristic fresh herbs. A great restaurant for dinner with a group of friends.

32 SUZIE Q
Dr. Lelykade 33-37
Scheveningen –
Harbour ⑤
+31 (0)70 743 36 76
restaurantsuzieq.nl

Trees, plants, wood, tiles. This hip restaurant is like an urban jungle in the harbour of Scheveningen. A romantic dinner, a lunch with a group of friends, a cocktail at the bar, a beer on the terrace with spectacular views, everything is possible. The menu is international with small plates to share. Great ambiance and friendly service.

33 TAPISCO

Kneuterdijk 11
Voorhout ②
+31 (0)70 204 50 06
restauranttapisco.nl

For this wine and small-plates restaurant, Michelin-starred chef and owner Marcel van der Kleijn went out of his way to create the cosmopolitan look and feel of present-day Spain and Portugal: hand-painted tiles from the Iberian Peninsula, calf leather couches from the USA. Additionally, by including a large bookcase he also paid tribute to the history of the building that for more than 300 years housed a bookshop.

34 PASTIS

Oude Molstraat 57
Hofkwartier ②
+31 (0)70 363 30 31
pastis.nl

Oh là là, this tiny bistro breathes Paris. The large aged mirrors, the mosaic floor, the marble bar top, the tightly spaced tables, the cafe chairs, the music, and, indeed, the French food: you'd almost forget that you are in The Hague! Do not expect fancy modern dishes, it's mostly the ambiance what makes this place special.

35 RESTAURANT CRU

Badhuisstraat 230
Scheveningen –
Visserijbuurt ⑤
+31 (0)6 26 10 50 32
restaurantcru.nl

Beautifully tiled, meat hooks and other butcher paraphernalia all around, and not to be missed: game in a dry-aging chamber. This restaurant is located in a 1900s butcher shop. This is the place to go for meat and game. All locally sourced and even hunted. Great entourage, great dishes, great wines.

Cafés

Café Express
Café Ristretto
Café Allonge
Cappuccino
Café au Lait
Nois...

The 5 best places to eat
FRESH FISH

36 WOX

Lange Voorhout 51
Voorhout ②
+31 (0)70 365 37 54
wox.nl

Restaurant Wox overlooks the most beautiful street in The Hague, the historical avenue Lange Voorhout. This large and chic restaurant is a golden oldie that serves elegant, modern and mostly fish-based dishes, often with an Asian touch: drunken lobster with sake, *sashimi hamachi* with coconut and black truffle, watercress salad with scallops and vanilla dressing.

37 BISTRO MER

Javastraat 9
Centrum ④
+31 (0)70 360 73 89
bistromer.nl

If you're in for a nostalgic night out, head to Bistro Mer. It's one of the most classic fish restaurants in town. The attractive oyster cart in front of the place, plus the art deco interior, make you feel like you are in the heart of Paris. As expected the menu is traditional French with dishes like Coquilles St Jacques and Sole à la Meunière.

38 COAST FISH

Prinsestraat 62
Hofkwartier ②
+31 (0)70 326 51 23

Looking for a place downtown to eat really good fish and chips? Go to this tiny shop annex eatery in the charming Prinsestraat. The fish burgers and fish croquettes are also worth trying. Coast Fish is the perfect place for a fish snack (with a glass of wine, if you like).

39 WATERPROEF

Dr. Lelykade 25
Scheveningen –
Harbour ⑤
+31 (0)70 358 87 70
restaurant
waterproef.nl

This restaurant is one of the most classy and stylish places in the harbour of Scheveningen. With many elegant and tasty fish dishes on the menu and an excellent wine list, it's a must for fish and wine lovers. On the first floor, you can enjoy an intimate tasting or dinner in the wine room amidst over 1000 unique bottles of wine.

40 SEAFOOD BAR VIGO

Aert van der
Goesstraat 9
Scheveningen –
Statenkwartier ③
+31 (0)70 205 02 73
restaurantvigo.nl

Vigo is in its place in the international Statenkwartier where many expats live. The international menu includes Japanese, Spanish, French, Italian as well as Dutch dishes. The fish is of high quality and the food is carefully presented. The interior is trendy and cosy with just the right amount of nautical decorations.

The 5 best spots for
INDONESIAN FOOD

---

41 **DAYANG**
Prinsestraat 65
Hofkwartier ②
+31 (0)70 364 99 79
eethuisdayang.nl

Tiny *toko*, but big in taste, Dayang has turned out dishes from Sumatra since 1996. On the menu, you'll find their specialities like *Empek-Empek Kapal Selam*, a fried fish fillet marinated in spicy sour sauce.

42 **TOKO BALI MANDIRA**
Abeelplein 3
Segbroek ⑧
+31 (0)70 363 38 91
tokobalimandera.nl

This family-run business builds on the legacy of Mrs. Ming, who became famous for her Indonesian snacks. She still is the force in the kitchen of this popular neighbourhood *toko*. The dishes at Toko Bali Mandera are super fresh and tasty. Like in the old days, the *rissoles* and *lempers* of Mrs. Ming are still their speciality.

43 **TOKO MENTENG**
Franse Kerkstraat 12
Voorburg ⑦
+31 (0)70 300 05 03
tokomenteng.nl

Among the best *tokos* in the Netherlands. Their kitchen is inspired by the cuisine of Java, one of the many Indonesian islands. True to the traditions and working with the freshest produce they can find, Toko Menteng never disappoints.

44 TOKO SAWA

**Frederik Hendrik-
laan 250
Scheveningen –
Statenkwartier ③
+31 (0)6 24 38 34 37**
tokosawa.nl

The Hague is famous for its small
Indonesian eateries, an inheritance of
the Dutch colonial past. At places like
Sawa, you can either sit and enjoy a meal
at one of the few tables, or order at the
counter for take-out. Sawa is praised for
its affordable fresh Javanese and Balinese
dishes. Alcohol is not served here.

45 KERATON DAMAI

**Groot Hertoginne-
laan 57
Scheveningen –
Duinoord ③
+31 (0)70 363 93 71**
keratondamai.nl

This traditional restaurant with wood-
carved wall panels serves enticing
Indonesian dishes in an authentic East
Javanese way. Order one of the rice tables
(a combination of several small dishes),
to get an impression of what this vibrant
cuisine has to offer. It's a small and
popular place, so book in advance!

5 casual places to enjoy
ASIAN CUISINE

46 **DE SUSHIMEISJES**
   Valkenboskade 622
   Segbroek ⑧
   +31 (0)70 737 04 03
   desushimeisjes.nl

De Sushimeisjes (Dutch for 'Sushi Girls') have several locations in The Hague, but this one at the Valkenboskade is the best for eating in. The large terrace is the place you want to be in summer while enjoying their inventive sushi. On the menu are many good vegetarian and vegan options.

47 **MR. BAP**
   Driehoekjes 37
   Hofkwartier ②
   +31 (0)6 41 76 47 21

This hidden 'hole in the wall' is not the kind of place for a first date, but if you are in the mood for a good Korean *bibimbap* with homemade *kimchi*, go to Mr. Bap. The owner, Mr. Bap himself, prepares delicious fresh Korean dishes in his tiny kitchen. This place, however, comes with a few handicaps: no pin, no toilets and no alcohol.

48 CURRY & COCOS

Prins Hendrik-
straat 83
Zeeheldenkwartier ③
+31 (0)70 360 26 00
curryencocos.nl

It can be busy with locals at this very informal Thai restaurant. On the menu are traditional and tasty Thai dishes like Tom Ka Kai, the famous chicken-coconut soup, and mains like Moe Pad Prik (spicy pork with basil) and Kung Nam Prik Pauw (shrimps in black curry). Its spicy papaya salad is also recommended.

49 ONI

Prinsestraat 35
Hofkwartier ②
+31 (0)70 364 52 40
oni-restaurant.nl

At this beautiful modern restaurant with coloured lights and wooden tables you can enjoy fancy Japanese dishes. They serve sushi and *sashimi*, of course, but also other tantalizing small dishes. Oni works with sustainable fish and has several good vegetarian options. Start the evening with one of their excellent cocktails.

50 RAMEN OHASHI

Weimarstraat 139
Segbroek ⑧
+31 (0)70 216 22 09

This small Japanese restaurant is named after the chef. Ohashi, who is from Tokyo, makes the famous Japanese ramen soup from scratch, even the noodles. On the menu are several variations: from the original ramen and *miso* ramen, to the thicker *tantanmen* ramen. Expect nothing fancy, just good food.

5 great
CHINESE
RESTAURANTS

---

51 **FAT KEE**
Gedempte Gracht 23
Chinatown ①
+31 (0)70 360 07 42
fatkee070.nl

Large portions, very affordable, and open until 1 am. No wonder that this low-key Chinese restaurant in Chinatown is immensely popular among people from the Chinese community, Dutch families, students, and tourists alike. No dim sum here, but large platters of Chinese dishes.

52 **FULL MOON CITY**
Achter Raamstraat 75
Chinatown ①
+31 (0)70 356 20 13
fullmooncity.nl

This restaurant in Chinatown is very popular within the Chinese community; obviously, a good sign. With its white paper tablecloths, red carpet and bright lighting, the decor is genuinely Chinese. The food is authentic, thus expect dishes such as dim sum, Cantonese barbecue and Chinese broth fondue.

53 **ZHENG**
Prinsestraat 33
Hofkwartier ②
+31 (0)70 362 08 28
restaurantzheng.com

Not for everyone's budget, this high-end Chinese restaurant in the Prinsestraat. The name refers to the copious Zheng banquet, an impressive meal that in Imperial China was served to important officials. You can enjoy the main Chinese cuisines here and choose between several elaborate menus with small elegant dishes.

54 MANDARIN PALACE

Nicolaistraat 35
Scheveningen –
Duinoord ③
+31 (0)70 360 66 16
mandarinpalace.nl

This Chinese gem, tucked away in a residential street, has been around for more than 20 years. Despite its age and in contrast with so many other Chinese restaurants, this place has a modern ambience and offers innovative, beautifully presented Chinese dishes. The steamed oysters with black bean sauce, the Peking duck pancakes and dim sum are among the best in town.

55 WINSTON & WEI WEI

Stationsweg 53
Stationsbuurt ①
+31 (0)70 326 39 30
winstonweiwei.com

Winston & Wei Wei started this small, unpretentious Chinese eatery some ten years ago. They offer Chinese food and kind service that are above average. In other words, Winston & Wei Wei has all the ingredients to make this Chinese restaurant one of the best in town. The canteen-like vibes only add to the charm and experience.

55 WINSTON & WEI WEI

5 relaxed places for good
ITALIAN FOOD

56 VINCENZO'S

Prins Hendrik-
straat 75
Zeeheldenkwartier ③
+31 (0)70 737 03 81
vincenzos.nl

The success of Vincenzo's has resulted in
the opening of several locations in town.
There is one to be found on the Denneweg, one in the Prinsestraat and one in the
Statenkwartier. The very first Vincenzo's
at the Prins Hendrikstraat, though, has
a special place in our heart. Here, the giant
wood oven occupies half of the restaurant.
Across the street, you'll find Vincenzo's
Osteria, a great place for pasta.

57 THAT'S AMORE

57 THAT'S AMORE

Laan van Meerder-
voort 188-A
Segbroek ⑧
+31 (0)70 324 70 90
thatsamore.nl

As soon as you open the door of That's Amore you find yourself in Italy. This informal deli with a few tables in the back can be busy during lunchtime. Neighbourhood residents love the panini, antipasti and simple pasta dishes here. Only open for lunch and take-out.

58 LA SORRENTINA

Molenstraat 19
Hofkwartier ②
+31 (0)70 785 62 46
lasorrentina.nl

An Italian-American couple opened this trattoria in one of the most picturesque streets of The Hague. The menu combines traditional dishes from Campania, the region where Laura Massa grew up, with Italian-inspired dishes by her American partner Michael: *Parmigiana di Nonna Laura, Rigatoni alla Siciliana,* but also Chicago-style Deep Dish Pizza.

59 PASTANINI

Frederik Hendrik-
laan 79
Scheveningen –
Statenkwartier ③
+31 (0)70 355 59 90
pastanini.com

If you are craving for a good authentic pizza, go to Pastanini. This always busy restaurant in the Statenkwartier has an enormous wood oven. Try to get a table in the more spacious back, or at the large marble bar if you like to watch how the Italian pizza chefs rapidly prepare the scrumptious pizzas.

60 CASA CAPELLO

Borneostraat 201
Archipel ④
+31 (0)70 225 03 03
casacapello.nl

The friendly neighbourhood restaurant Casa Capello specialises in traditional food from Piemonte. They make fresh pasta. It is praised for its *antipasti* and *primi,* like roasted peppers with garlic-parsley sauce with anchovies and *caserecce al pesto con stracciatella.*

The 5 best
NEIGHBOURHOOD
RESTAURANTS

---

61 CAFÉ FRANKLIN
Valkenbosplein 24
Segbroek ⑧
+31 (0)70 785 14 12
cafefranklin.nl

Hip decor, great beers, friendly service, and pub food that is better than anywhere else: Café Franklin is a beloved place in the neighbourhood. On the menu are good bar snacks like *Flammkuchen*, pork belly buns and oysters, and mains such as sticky pork ribs, fish tacos and burgers.

62 DE TAPPERIJ
Atjehstraat 66
Archipel ④
+31 (0)70 352 39 98
*restaurant
detapperij.nl*

With Balinese masks, paintings and paraphernalia on the wall, the interior of this restaurant is quite eclectic. A large part of the beautiful dark wooden interior, though, dates back to 1886. Once a cafe, now a classic but informal restaurant with many French and some Indonesian dishes on the menu.

63 CAFÉ CONSTANT
Neptunusstraat 2
Visserijbuurt ⑤
+31 (0)70 412 77 72
cafeconstant.nl

Reviews from both customers and professionals hail the quality of the food, service and atmosphere at Café Constant, a small and simply decorated restaurant in old town Scheveningen. Expect lots of taste, organic produce and some great vegetarian options. The sunny terrace is a bonus.

64 LORELEI

Regentesseplein 11
Segbroek ⑧
+31 (0)70 744 39 72
loreleicafe.nl

This part of the Regentessekwartier is working hard to become hip and happening and this new modern bar-restaurant is a welcome addition to this. It's a place where locals meet for a drink, a bite and a chat in the bright but cosy restaurant, or, when the sun is out, on the large terrace on the square. The international menu has something for every taste.

65 CAFÉ AIMÉE

Lijsterbesplein 2
Segbroek ⑧
+31 (0)70 250 52 39
cafe-aimee.nl

This new restaurant, with its dark botanic atmosphere, velvet sofas and cosy terrace, has nothing to do with the stuffy old pub that was located here before. Most neighbourhood residents are happy with the metamorphose. Now they can have lunch or dinner, enjoying international modern dishes.

61 CAFÉ FRANKLIN

The 5 best places to
EAT AT THE BEACH

---

66 STRANDPAVILJOEN ZUID
Zuiderstrand 3,
Strandslag 11
Segbroek ⑤
+31 (0)6 16 92 67 83
strandpaviljoen-zuid.nl

Located at the so-called 'silent beach', this is one of the most laidback beach pavilions to start or end your day. Wake up slowly with a breakfast board with Turkish bread, frittata, organic cheese, yoghurt and fresh fruit, or watch the sun go down in the sea while enjoying a spit-roasted chicken or a stone-oven pizza.

67 DE STAAT

67 DE STAAT

Zuiderstrand 4,
Strandslag 10
Loosduinen ⑤
+31 (0)70 338 88 60
destaat.info

With its Adirondack chairs in the sand, this is a great place to eat while enjoying the sunset. De Staat is well known for its 'Staatsplateau', a large mouth-watering appetiser board (a vegetarian version is also available). On windy days, this is also a great place to spot kite surfers.

68 NATUREL

Noorderstrand 2,
Zwarte Pad
Scheveningen –
Beach ⑤
+31 (0)6 81 28 39 07
naturel.info

Off the beaten track and 'natural' in every way. This relaxed beach pavilion is located at a nude beach (although *au naturel* eating is not permitted). It serves dishes with organic and free-range ingredients, and the interior is made of natural materials. It has many healthy and creative dishes on the menu.

69 DE KWARTEL

Zuiderstrand,
Strandslag 9
Loosduinen ⑤
+31 (0)70 355 56 15
dekwartel.nl

It might not be the hippest beach pavilion, but the impressive wine list with more than 100 wines makes this a unique place. A big plus: the kitchen works with organic meat and the menu has many vegetarian options.

70 HET PUNTJE

At the far end
of Noorderstrand,
Zwarte Pad
Scheveningen –
Beach ⑤
+31 (0)6 83 71 21 98
strandtenthetpuntje.nl

Head to this friendly beach pavilion if you want to escape the tourist crush of Scheveningen boulevard. It takes some effort to reach it, but you'll be rewarded with peace and quiet and a simple but tasty meal. The small menu changes regularly, but always includes vegetarian options.

The 5 best spots for
A QUICK BITE

---

71 BURGER BAR
Plein 3
Old Centre ①
+31 (0)70 213 60 38
burgerbar.nl

Burger fans go to the Burger Bar. Here you can choose your own high-quality beef (Irish, Angus or Wagyu), your own bun, and select your toppings (put a fried egg on top!). With two succulent no-meat burgers on the menu, this fast-casual restaurant is also kind to vegetarians.

72 KING FALAFEL
Vlamingstraat 37
Old Centre ①
+31 (0)70 427 58 61
kingfalafel.nl

Although this place has the name and looks of a fast-food chain, it's a one-off, family-run eatery. You can either eat a falafel sandwich or baked potato. At the bar, you can add all the scrumptious toppings of your liking yourself, like garlicky yoghurt, hummus, salads, vegetables and spicy sauces.

73 BALADI MANOUCHE
Torenstraat 95
Hofkwartier ②
+31 (0)70 444 38 77
baladionline.nl

A great little 'hole in the wall' where you can get authentic Lebanese street food. The owner is from Beirut and prepares his *man'ouches* (flatbreads) in the traditional way. The dough is homemade and comes with various toppings, such as *za'atar*, homemade yoghurt, white cheese, and minced beef.

74 WARUNG MINI

Amsterdamse
Veerkade 57-A
Chinatown ①
+31 (0)70 365 46 28
warungminidenhaag.nl

The Hague has a large Dutch-Surinam community and Surinam restaurants can be found all over town. Warung Mini, which serves Surinam-Indonesian food, is a popular place for a quick Surinam sandwich, a *roti* (flatbread with potatoes, meat or veggies) or *saoto* (chicken soup).

75 BAKKERIJ MAXIMA

Prins Hendrik-
straat 78
Zeeheldenkwartier ③
+31 (0)70 345 30 23

For the best Turkish pizzas (*lahamcum*) and döner kebabs, go to this Turkish bakery. Besides pizza and döner kebab, it also sells *borek* (a filo pastry pie filled with cheese and spinach or ground meat), baklava, *simit* (circular bread), and much more. Everything is homemade and fresh. No seats.

73 BALADI MANOUCHE

The 5 best places to enjoy
DUTCH HERRING

---

76 **HARINGKAR HARTEVELD**

Corner Reinkenstraat / Obrechtstraat Scheveningen – Duinoord ③
+31 (0)6 14 41 79 29

On Thursdays, Fridays and Saturdays you'll find the Harteveld family working hard to clean and prepare herrings for all the loyal and hungry customers. This stall has been around for more than 25 years and the friendly owners know many of the regulars by their names. It's the most charming place for a herring in town.

76 HARINGKAR HARTEVELD

77 HARINGKRAAM BUITENHOF

Buitenhof 22 (near the Hofvijver)
Voorhout ②
+31 (0)70 365 79 60

Who doesn't want to eat a Dutch herring while overlooking the beautiful Hofvijver (Court Pond) and the 'Little Tower' where the Dutch Prime Minister has his office? You can have great herring here and might even bump into a minister or a member of parliament.

78 SIMONIS AAN DE HAVEN

Visafslag 20
Scheveningen –
Harbour ⑤
+31 (0)70 350 00 42
simonisvis.nl

The well-known Simonis 'fish family' owns several fish restaurants in town, from basic to quite glamourous. This location at Scheveningen harbour is informal and, therefore, a great place to devour a herring. When the famous New Dutch Herring (de Hollandse Nieuwe) is in season, there is a herring stall outside.

79 HET HARINGHUISJE

Vissershavenweg 66
Scheveningen –
Harbour ⑤
+31 (0)70 355 67 24
hetharinghuisje.nl

Het Haringhuisje (meaning: little herring house) is one of the best places for a Dutch herring. Traditionally, in The Hague herring is eaten by holding it by its tail and letting the fish slide into your mouth. If this makes you feel uncomfortable, you can have it on a bun or eat it the Amsterdam way: cut into pieces and with a cocktail stick.

80 VISHANDEL DE LANGE

Marcelisstraat 37-B
Scheveningen –
Beach ⑤
+31 (0)70 404 97 07
viswinkeldelange.nl

This little fishmonger is tucked away in a residential street in Scheveningen, but herring and fish lovers know to find it. The owner Ben de Lange sometimes organises workshops 'how to clean a herring', because he doesn't want this tradition to be lost.

5 excellent
ICE-CREAM SHOPS

81 **HET IJSKABINET**
Plaats 31
Hofkwartier ②
ijskabinet.nl

Opened only recently, Het IJskabinet is already a favourite among locals, and because of the vicinity of the House of Representatives you might bump into a member of parliament as well. It's hard to choose from the wide variety of home-made flavours. The hazelnut and pistachio flavours are pure and delicious.

82 **LA VENEZIA**
Laan van Meerdervoort 596
Segbroek ⑧
+31 (0)70 363 69 93

La Venezia is wonderfully old-fashioned. This little ice-cream shop is now run by third-generation Italians and neither the decor nor the recipes seem to have changed much since its opening in 1934. Expect traditional ice-cream flavours of good quality here.

83 **FLORENCIA**
Torenstraat 55
Hofkwartier ②
+31 (0)70 363 02 14
florenciaijs.nl

This large parlour, run by the Talamini family since 1932, is not just a place where people go for an ice cream or a cheap coffee, it's also a place where locals hang out and discuss politics, sports and world events. Taxi drivers, construction workers, diplomats and civil servants: everyone loves the place.

84 LUCIANO

Theresiastraat 41
Haagse Hout ⑥
+31 (0)70 415 87 57
ijssalonluciano.nl

Luciano sells high-quality ice cream made with fresh fruits and natural ingredients. On sunny days, people gather here to taste the unique flavours Luciano is famous for, such as honey-and-fig or raspberry-crumble. You can also drink a good cup of coffee here, served with a mini ice-cream cone instead of a cookie. A smaller Luciano shop can be found on Frederik Hendriklaan 230-B.

85 PIET ARTISANS OF FLAVOUR

Piet Heinstraat 76
Zeeheldenkwartier ④

This new, hip ice-cream parlour offers original flavours, such as *halva*, mint-lemon-ginger, sticky rice and coconut, and *chai masala*. What makes it especially modern, is that it has many vegan options. Its fruit comes directly from neighbouring greengrocer Rutten. They're willing to let you taste before you choose.

81 HET IJSKABINET

85 PIET ARTISANS OF FLAVOUR

5
LOCAL SPECIALITIES
you must try

---

86 HAAGSCHE KAKKER

AT: BAKKERIJ HESSING
Denneweg 186
Voorhout ②
+31 (0)70 737 05 52
gebakbestellen
denhaag.nl

The Haagsche Kakker, also known as the 'Haagsche Krentenkakker' is a famous treat from The Hague. This raisin bread-cake filled with a buttery cinnamon-almond paste is an invention of the Hessing bakery. *Krentenkakker* is Dutch for a wealthy cheapskate. It is sometimes said that The Hague is the city where many *krentenkakkers* live, hence the name.

87 SHRIMP CROQUETTES

AT: VISHANDEL
ZOUTENBIER
Groot Hertoginne-
laan 147
Scheveningen –
Duinoord ③
+31 (0)70 345 11 73

For almost fifty years, this fishmonger has been famous for its homemade shrimp croquettes. At lunchtime, it can be crowded here with people waiting for their freshly baked croquettes. Crunchy on the outside, soft and creamy on the inside. The croquettes are made from scratch and based on an old, secret family recipe.

88 GENEVERS, LIQUEURS, BITTERS

AT: VAN KLEEF
Lange Beesten-markt 109
Old Centre ①
+31 (0)70 345 22 73
museumvankleef.nl

The Van Kleef distillery, founded in 1842, is still in use today, albeit as a cafe annex distillery museum. The quality of the Dutch genevers, liqueurs and bitters produced by Van Kleef – based on the original recipes – is outstanding. A visit to the former distillery is a must. It's as if you are entering a cafe from another era. Book a tasting!

89 MONASTERY BEER

AT: BROUWERIJ HAAGSCHE BROEDER
Oude Molstraat 35
Hofkwartier ②
haagschebroeder.nl
monasticstore.nl

The Hague is blessed with its own monastery beer. It's made in the Monastery of the Brothers of Saint John, situated in the historic centre. At this microbrewery, the Brothers brew around 1000 litres a week, including some special editions. Their beer is served in several beer cafes in town and sold in large bottles in the monastery shop.

90 MEATBALL SANDWICH

AT: DUNGELMANN
Hoogstraat 17
Hofkwartier ②
+31 (0)70 346 23 00
slagerijdungelmann.nl

Almost every resident of The Hague has had Dungelmann's *broodje bal* at least once in his or her life. This butcher's shop has been around for over 150 years and has been serving meatballs to its clientele ever since. Voted best meatball sandwich of The Hague many times over, it's a must-eat while in The Hague.

BOOKSTOR

45 PLACES TO GO FOR A DRINK

---

5 places with **EXCEPTIONAL COFFEE** —————— 64

The 5 most **CHARMING COFFEE BARS** ———— 66

The 5 best **CAFES WHERE YOU CAN READ OR WORK** *(and drink coffee)* ————————— 68

The 5 best places for **(HIGH) TEA** ——————— 70

5 cafes with **FABULOUS TERRACES** —————— 72

The 5 best **BEER BARS** ———————————— 75

5 great places for a **GOOD GLASS OF WINE** — 77

5 cool places to enjoy **A COCKTAIL** ————— 79

The 5 best bars to **DRINK WITH THE LOCALS** — 82

5 places with
EXCEPTIONAL COFFEE

---

91 KAAFI

Prinsestraat 25
Hofkwartier ②
+31 (0)6 11 77 66 10
kaafi.nl

The owner lived in London before opening this modern coffee bar with jazzy vibes. He gets his house blend from a London roaster and takes the art of coffee seriously. But just to mention the coffee does the kitchen injustice: the cakes, made by his mom, are out of this world! Kaafi is also popular for its scrumptious food.

92 SINGLE ESTATE COFFEE ROASTERS – DE BAR

Piet Heinstraat 15
Zeeheldenkwartier ④
+31 17 453 53 03
singleestatecoffee.nl

After a couple of years searching for the best beans, processing methods and roasting profiles, this speciality coffee roaster opened its uber-hip coffee bar in a beautiful old corner building. Drink superb coffee in the black and wood interior with plants.

93 TIGERSHARK

Badhuisstraat 114
Scheveningen –
Visserijbuurt ⑤
+31 (0)6 24 44 59 00
tigersharkcoffee.nl

Surfers, young parents, neighbourhood residents, they all love to hang out at Tigershark in Scheveningen. No wonder, since the coffee at this relaxed coffee bar is made with love and attention. Tigershark gets its high-quality beans from micro-roaster Shokunin, based in Rotterdam.

94 FILTRO

Papestraat 11
Hofkwartier ②
+31 (0)6 42 84 70 73
filtro.coffee

Great atmosphere, friendly staff, and most important: excellent coffee. The owner imports the roasted beans from the Danish La Cabra Coffee Roasters. The aromatic, floral and delicate taste of the coffee stands out. Do not forget to order a piece of the amazing homemade cakes, which are made with honey instead of sugar.

95 CAPRIOLE CAFÉ

Fokkerkade 18
Laak ⑦
+31 (0)70 701 10 10
capriolecafe.nl

A cool restaurant/coffee bar located in a former paint factory in the increasingly trendy Binckhorst. The fair trade and organic coffee beans are roasted in house. The baristas prepare you all kinds of coffee, from a simple and always double espresso to an espresso with pink peppercorns, a cappuccino *brûlée*, an *affogato*, and much more.

95 CAPRIOLE CAFÉ

The 5 most
CHARMING
COFFEE BARS

---

96 **BOOKSTOR**
   Noordeinde 39
   Hofkwartier ②
   +31 (0)70 326 57 90
   bookstor.nl

Coffee, cake, books! Read and drink coffee in this former legal bookshop. Surrounded by old bookcases with new and secondhand books, plants and vintage furniture this is one of the best places to lose yourself in a good book and an excellent coffee. In summer, the large terrace and the garden are wonderful to relax.

97 **LOLA BIKES**
   AND COFFEE
   Noordeinde 91
   Hofkwartier ②
   +31 (0)6 29 08 77 93
   lolabikesandcoffee.nl

A coffee bar in a bike shop, or maybe it's the other way around. Fact is that you can enjoy a great coffee while admiring the bikes and everything bike around you. Lola has its own cycling community. Several times a week, a cycling group departs from its premises.

98 FLEUR'S

Van Bylandtstraat 92
Segbroek ⑧
+31 (0)70 216 08 98
fleurs-koffie.nl

This delightful tiny coffee bar feels a bit like a neighbourhood living room, where you meet with friends for a good cup of coffee or a simple lunch. The owners prefer to work with local businesses: the coffee is roasted by the Roast Factory, the bread comes from Lekker Brood and the cheese from Ed Boele.

99 WIENER KONDITOREI

Korte Poten 24
Voorhout ②
+31 (0)70 360 05 49
wienerkonditorei.nl

Not hip at all, but instead a place where time has stood still. Since 1934, this small well-known coffee house has been specialising in Viennese coffee and pastries like *Apfelstrudel, Sachertorte* and *Bundt* cake. The founders introduced the first espresso machine to The Hague, which they brought with them from a trip to Vienna.

100 POMPKE

Pompstationweg 2
(corner Doornikse-
straat)
Scheveningen –
Belgisch Park ⑤
pompke.nl

Pompke is situated in a tiny 'coffee house', a kiosk where labourers used to go for a cheap cup of coffee. These kinds of kiosks, also known as *koffiehuizen,* are typical of The Hague. Pompke is still a coffee house, but after its facelift, it's also a charming neighbourhood hang-out where you can get good coffee and homemade cakes.

The 5 best
CAFES WHERE YOU CAN READ OR WORK
(and drink coffee)

---

101 **DUDOK**
Hofweg 1-A
Old Centre ①
+31 (0)70 890 01 00
dudok.nl

This timeless grand cafe-restaurant right across the parliament buildings is the perfect location for a business appointment. With a large communal table, it's also a good place to read the paper or do some work on your laptop. Of course, not without ordering a coffee and a piece of the renowned Dudok apple pie.

102 **COFFEE WORKS**
Parkweg 56
Voorburg ⑦
+31 (0)70 216 65 15
coffee-works.nl

The interior of this place in the historic centre of Voorburg is cosy and retro. There is a bright room in the back where you can plug in your laptop. In summer, you can watch sheep grazing on the green meadow in front of the Old Church across the street.

103 **PERRON X COFFEE ROASTERS**
Torenstraat 98
Old Centre ①
+31 (0)6 36 04 25 67
perronxcoffee.nl

This Hague-based coffee roaster recently took over the coffee bar opposite the Hague Tower of the Grote Kerk. A relaxed and spacy bar where you can work and drink good coffee at the same time.

104 CENTRAL LIBRARY
Spui 68
Old Centre ①
+31 (0)70 353 44 55
bibliotheekdenhaag.nl

Working with a view! The recently remodelled public library has a cafe on the fifth floor where you can quietly read a book or sit with your laptop while overlooking the Spui area. Besides coffee, it offers some small dishes like grilled cheese sandwiches, cakes and cookies.

105 HOUSE OF TRIBES
Turfmarkt 28
Uilebomen ②
+31 (0)70 205 02 20
houseoftribes.nl

Mellow music, really good coffee, a large community table, and many outlets to charge your laptop. Next to Campus The Hague of Leiden University and some large ministries, this casual coffee bar is mostly frequented by students and civil servants. If you do not feel like working: this place has a laptop-free zone as well.

105 HOUSE OF TRIBES

The 5 best places for
(HIGH) TEA

---

106 HUG THE TEA

Papestraat 13
Hofkwartier ②
+31 (0)6 38 71 05 93
hugthetea.com

Claire and Lisa, the 'tea sisters', have
been huge fans of the green, powdery
matcha tea for years. In 2015, they
decided to open a tea bar specialised in
their favourite Japanese tea. It was an
instant hit with tea lovers. Hug the Tea
also offers a breakfast and lunch menu.
Try the matcha smoothie bowls and
matcha pancakes!

106 HUG THE TEA

107 BLOSSOM

**Anna Paulowna-
straat 70-C**
Zeeheldenkwartier ④
+31 (0)70 211 18 13
cafeblossom.nl

The homemade cakes of this casual daytime restaurant are simply irresistible! And the teas they serve are from the high-quality and well-known brand Crusio. This makes Blossom a great place for a cup of tea with a sweet treat. If you like it more festive: Blossom also organises high teas (reservations only).

108 HOTEL DES INDES

Lange Voorhout 54-56
Voorhout ②
+31 (0)70 361 23 45
*hoteldesindes
thehague.com*

Why not have a high tea in the lounge of the most legendary hotel of The Hague? While enjoying a four-course high tea you can catch a glimpse of the luxurious and exuberantly styled hotel. Famous men and women stayed here: from president Eisenhower, Eleanor Roosevelt and Audrey Hepburn to Josephine Baker, Prince and The Rolling Stones.

109 HIGH TEA BOAT

VARIOUS PICK-UP AND
DROP-OFF OPTIONS
Old Centre
Hofkwartier
Voorhout
+31 (0)6 44 44 29 68
bootvarendenhaag.nl

The most romantic high tea in town! Enjoy good-quality tea (Betjeman & Barton) and scrumptious homemade cakes and sandwiches with friends on an open boat while gliding through the beautiful canals and along the green parks of The Hague. For groups of 10 people or more.

110 OP Z'N KOP

Prinsestraat 112
Hofkwartier ②
+31 (0)6 81 02 90 18

Amidst old French mirrors, English tables, closets filled with china, plants and small presents – all for sale, the owner has put seats and tables where you can enjoy a cup of tea and homemade pies. High tea by appointment only.

5 cafes with
FABULOUS TERRACES

111 GEMBER

Stadhouderslaan 43
Scheveningen –
Zorgvliet ③
+31 (0)70 358 68 91
restaurantgember.nl

This daytime restaurant belongs to the museum building where also the GEM and the Photography Museum are located. The sun-drenched terrace of this modern museum restaurant is just splendid! Drink a coffee or have a glass of wine while overlooking the pond and the adjacent Kunstmuseum, one of the best works of architect Berlage.

112 ROOM

Anna Paulowna-
plein 16
Zeeheldenkwartier ④
+31 (0)70 363 00 02
roomdenhaag.com

As soon as the sun is out, the terrace of Room is filled with cheerful sun lovers. This relaxed cafe-restaurant with terrace is located on the charming Anna Paulownaplein. Under the trees, you can enjoy breakfast, lunch or dinner. Or just have a drink accompanied by a plate of delicious appetisers.

111 GEMBER

115 LA RANA

113 PALMETTE

Plaats 27
Hofkwartier ②
+31 (0)70 412 75 12
palmette.nl

Until the 18th century, Plaats was the square where public executions took place. Now it's a cheerful place with shops and restaurants, like Palmette. In summer, the terrace of this bar-restaurant is one of the most historical places for a coffee or a drink, while admiring the façades of the surrounding old buildings and the medieval prison gate.

114 GREENS

AT: WESTBROEKPARK
Kapelweg 18
Scheveningen –
Westbroekpark ⑤
+31 (0)70 369 53 73
greensinthepark.nl

In a newly built greenhouse in the middle of Westbroekpark, you can enjoy coffee, drinks and organic dishes made with veggies from the vegetable garden, also to be found on the property. The lush secluded terrace is one of the best places to relax. Greens also organises 'green' events, like organic theatre dinners, barbecues with garden salads, and garden days.

115 LA RANA

Stationsweg 42-44
Stationsbuurt ①
+31 (0)6 15 66 57 09
barlarana.nl

This Spanish wine bar with a modern take on tapas has a beautiful large terrace on the Huygenspark. La Rana has been there for ages, but was recently taken over by new owners who have unrecognisably updated it in every aspect. On the menu are interesting dishes, such as fennel salad with a yoghurt-limoncello dressing and fried cauliflower with *romesco* sauce. Great vibes!

The 5 best
BEER BARS

---

116 HOPPZAK
Papestraat 26-A
Hofkwartier ②
+31 (0)70 744 96 73

One of the cosiest places for beer in town. This beautiful bar is tucked away in an old cellar. You can choose from 15 to 20 draft beers and about 200 bottled beers. In addition to beer, it has a cool selection of whiskies and spirits as well. Live jazz and blues jam sessions on Thursday nights!

117 KOMPAAN CRAFT BEER BAR
Saturnusstraat 55
Laak ⑦
+31 (0)70 762 24 94
kompaanbier.nl

Urban, rough, and a hit ever since its opening in 2015. Kompaan is the most famous craft beer brand of The Hague, and the best place to drink it, is at its own brewery and bar in the industrial park the Binckhorst. With 20 beers on tap and a large sun-drenched terrace, this bar is totally relaxing.

118 CAFÉ DE LA GARE
Nieuwe School-
straat 13-A
Voorhout ②
+31 (0)70 744 62 55
delagare.nl

With more than 200 kinds of speciality beers, this informal bar is a favourite hang-out for local beer lovers. Owner Lambert Willems has a talent for figuring out what his customers like. Among the beers are some unique collaborations and one-offs. In summer, the sun-drenched terrace is the perfect place for a beer.

119 VAN KINSBERGEN
**Prins Hendrik-
plein 15
Zeeheldenkwartier** ③
+31 (0)70 310 78 92
*gastropub
vankinsbergen.nl*

A large gastropub and a microbrewery. Since its opening in 2018, Van Kinsbergen is the new darling of the residents of the hip Zeeheldenkwartier. Besides its own Van Kinsbergen Pale Ale brew, the pub has a large selection of imported, Belgian and Dutch beers. Beer tastings for small groups available.

120 DE PAAS
**Dunne Bierkade 16-A
Chinatown** ①
+31 (0)70 360 00 19
depaas.nl

The location of this beer pub at the Bierkade (beer quay) couldn't have been more appropriate. With more than 10 beers on tap and 174 bottled beers this is a must-visit for beer fanatics. The terrace boat in front of the pub is one of the most picturesque places for a drink in town.

117 KOMPAAN CRAFT BEER BAR

5 great places for a
GOOD GLASS OF WINE

---

121 GRAPES & OLIVES
Veenkade 1
Zeeheldenkwartier ④
+31 (0)70 346 66 82
grapesandolives.nl

This canal-side enoteca serves small plates and has a good selection of mostly Mediterranean wines. The best place for a drink and a bite is on the large terrace boat on the canal. Or grab a bar table by the open window. It's a great place for a pre-dinner glass of wine or an informal meal with friends.

122 LAPSANG
Oude Molstraat 11-A
Hofkwartier ②
+31 (0)70 360 35 98
lapsang.nl

A lunch- and tearoom during the day, a wine bar in the evening. This cute informal place is shared by two owners. Both are great in their own way, but if you are craving for a good glass of wine, accompanied by enticing small plates to share, stop by after 5 pm.

123 LE CAFÉ
Oude Molstraat 26-A
Hofkwartier ②
+31 (0)70 360 40 55
le-cafe.nl

This intimate and casual place is always packed. People gather here to have an excellent glass of wine or a traditional French bistro meal at one of the small tables in the back. The vibes are very relaxed with enjoyable music, friendly staff and many neighbourhood residents. Book ahead if you want to have dinner here.

124 BOUZY, WINE & FOOD

Denneweg 83
Voorhout ②
+31 (0)70 780 35 63
bouzywineandfood.nl

Locals love to hang out here after work for a good glass of wine and a selection of small bites. The location at the historical Denneweg and the informal interior add to the charm of this wine bar, that has a great selection of wines by the glass.

125 DE KADE

Dunne Bierkade 1-A
Chinatown ①
+31 (0)70 889 33 30
dekade.online

You could (and should) come here for the great natural wine selection and the sustainable food menu, since there are few places as environmentally literate as De Kade. Should that alone not be enough reason to stop by, then the terrace certainly is: linger in the sun alongside the centuries-old canal enjoying a bite and a drink, even from a sun chair if you're lucky.

125 DE KADE

5 cool places to enjoy
A COCKTAIL

────────────

126 VAVOOM TIKI ROOM

Grote Markt 30
Old Centre ①
+31 (0)70 346 75 06
vavoomtikiroom.nl

The vibes are tropical for sure at this popular and somewhat kitsch tiki bar. The cocktail list is long with – of course – the best rum-based creations. The drinks are made by skilled and fun-to-watch bartenders who pour your mix in a typical tiki mug if you like (10 euro deposit for this retro experience).

127 THE FIVE POINTS

Korte Houtstraat 5-A
Uilebomen ②
thefivepointsbar.nl

A classy and relaxed bar for discerning cocktail drinkers. The owner and bartender Michael Ziengs gained experience in 'cocktail city' London and then opened an intimate bar in downtown The Hague. Together with his bartender colleague he now creates the most beautiful and tasty cocktails.

128 BLEYENBERG

Grote Markt 10
Old Centre ①
+31 (0)70 800 21 20
bleyenbergdenhaag.nl

The relaxed rooftop bar at Bleyenberg is young, trendy and perfect for a cocktail. Thursday night is cocktail night: bartenders create a special edition cocktail and all cocktails cost 7,50 euro. The cocktail bar is on the third floor and from the terrace you'll have great views over the Grote Markt (a lively square) and the Grote Kerk (the church).

129 ULTRAMARIJN

Kneuterdijk 8
Voorhout ②
+31 (0)70 218 57 05
ultramarijnbar.nl

In the former-bank-turned-hotel Voco, cocktail bar Ultramarijn mixes original cocktails from all over the world using local and sustainable ingredients where possible. Do not expect the classics, but let yourself be pleasantly surprised by the knowledgeable bartenders.

130 BRICKS 'HOOCH & BREW'

Prinsestraat 5-A
Hofkwartier ②
+31 (0)6 15 23 21 80
bricksbar.nl

This large urban cocktail bar has a 'no menu' concept. The very skilled and energetic bartenders just ask for your preferences and start mixing, shaking, stirring with all available tools... It's magical! The drinks they put in front of you do not only please the eye but also the palate. The team really have a gift to figure out what you like.

The 5 best bars to
DRINK WITH
THE LOCALS

---

131 HUPPEL THE PUB
Oude Molstraat 21
Hofkwartier ②
+31 (0)70 360 91 13
dehuppel.nl

This lively pub has won the award of best cafe of the Netherlands in 2018. With its impressive collection of whiskies displayed behind the bar, many speciality beers on draft (including the pub's own HuppALE), this is a place where locals, students, civil servants and tourists feel at home.

132 CAFÉ DE KLEINE WITTE
Mallemolen 31
Willemspark ④
+31 (0)70 360 13 27
cafedekleinewitte.nl

For an authentic Dutch pub experience, go to De Kleine Witte. It's the place where the young and the old, the real estate agent and the taxi driver come together for a drink. The interior of this old pub is genuinely Dutch with Persian rugs on the tables, old leather bar stools and a pool table.

133 LOKAAL DUINOORD
Obrechtstraat 198
Scheveningen –
Duinoord ③
+31 (0)70 743 00 00
lokaalduinoord.nl

Locals and expats love this small Dutch pub in Duinoord. The staff are friendly and the beer selection is great with six beers on draft and 60 bottled beers. Lokaal also serves very decent pub food. It gets its meat from one of the best butchers in town: 't Oude Ambacht.

134 CAFÉ DE OUDE MOL

Oude Molstraat 61
Hofkwartier ②
+31 (0)70 345 16 23

If you're looking for the definition of 'cosy', visit the intimate and welcoming Café de Oude Mol. This tiny cafe with its eclectic, bohemian interior is for the young and the old, the locals and the passers-by. Live music on Monday, tapas from Wednesday through Saturday and always a great selection of beers.

135 CAFÉ DE SIEN

Antonie Heinsius-
straat 39
Scheveningen –
Statenkwartier ③
+31 (0)70 355 55 66
desien.nl

This pub is situated in the Staten-kwartier, a residential area close to many international organisations, where the majority of expats have settled. Locals and foreigners meet and relax at De Sien, to drink a good draft beer after work or eat a simple pub meal. The homemade shrimp croquettes and cheese fondue are favourites.

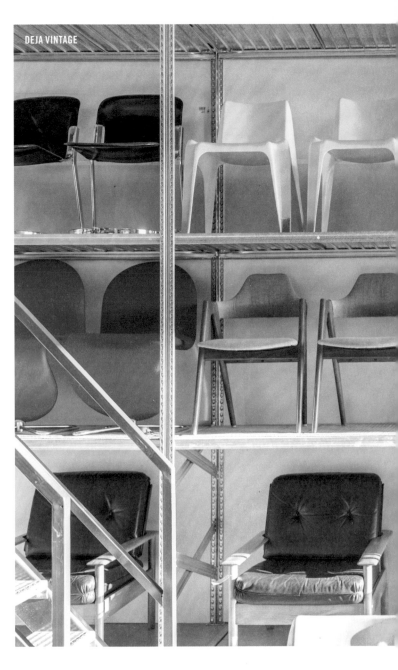

115 PLACES
TO SHOP

The 5 cosiest MARKETS —————————— 88

5 excellent CHEESE SHOPS —————————— 90

5 mouth-watering DELIS ————————— 92

5 amazing places for BREAD, PASTRY and
PATISSERIE ————————————— 94

5 great shops to buy TEA OR COFFEE ————— 96

5 indispensable shops to buy CHOCOLATE ———— 98

The 5 best NON-WESTERN FOOD shops ——— 100

5 special WINE BOUTIQUES ——————— 102

The 5 best SPECIALITY SHOPS——————— 104

5 great VINTAGE & RETRO
INTERIOR SHOPS ————————————— 106

The 5 best LIFESTYLE &
CONCEPT STORES ————————————— 109

The 5 best **FURNITURE & HOME DECORATION** *shops* —————— 111

The 5 best **GIFT SHOPS** —————— 114

The 5 most inspiring **JEWELLERY SHOPS** —————— 116

5 great shops to buy **VINTAGE & SECONDHAND CLOTHING** —————— 118

The 5 best **FASHION BOUTIQUES FOR HER** —————— 120

The 5 best **FASHION BOUTIQUES FOR HIM** —————— 122

5 places to buy special **SHOES** —————— 124

The 5 best **BOOKSHOPS** —————— 126

The 5 most inspiring **ART GALLERIES** *and* **ART RENTALS** —————— 128

The 5 best **SURF & SKATE** *shops* —————— 130

5 **LOCAL DESIGNERS** *to check out* —————— 132

5 charming shops to buy **FLOWERS & PLANTS** —————— 134

The 5 cosiest
MARKETS

———————————

136 DE HAAGSE MARKT

Herman Costerstraat
Schilderswijk ⑨
dehaagsemarkt.nl

Discover the eclectic mix of cultures at one of the largest outdoor markets in Europe. At this market, you'll find Dutch cheese, tropical fruits and vegetables, Turkish olives and *baklava*, Surinam *roti*, and much more. Do not miss the fresh fish stands where vendors extol their wares loudly. Open on Monday, Wednesday, Friday and Saturday.

137 LE MARIE MARCHÉ

Plein
Voorhout ②
lemariemarche.nl

Who doesn't long for a stroll over a romantic market in the sunny South of France from time to time? Where you can slurp oysters, eat *fromage*, drink wine and champagne, buy delicatessen, French gifts and *brocante*? Le Marie Marché brings this charming French atmosphere to The Hague every month.

138 ORGANIC MARKET

Lange Voorhout
Voorhout ②

Every Wednesday from 10 am to 6 pm, you can find this organic market at Lange Voorhout. The friendly stallholders at this small and charming market sell only the best of fruits, veggies, cheeses, breads and meats.

139 ANTIQUE AND BOOK MARKET

Lange Voorhout
Voorhout ②
*haagseantiek
enboekenmarkt.nl*

This antique and book market with more than seventy stalls located at the most beautiful avenue in The Hague has been held since 1971. Here you can find anything from rare books and records to old postcards, antique silverware, globes and curiosities. Open from mid-May to end of September on Thursdays and Sundays.

140 ROYAL CHRISTMAS FAIR

Lange Voorhout
Voorhout ②
royalchristmasfair.nl

With more than one hundred festive stalls, The Hague has one of the biggest Christmas markets in the Netherlands. The location is royal for sure, as the fair takes place at the Lange Voorhout where the idyllic winter palace of Queen Emma (great-grandmother of King Willem-Alexander) is situated.

138 ORGANIC MARKET

5 *excellent*
CHEESE SHOPS

141 KAASSPECIAALZAAK ED BOELE

Fahrenheitstraat 625
Segbroek ⑧
+31 (0)70 363 18 19
kaasspeciaalzaak.nl

For anyone who loves cheese, this place is heaven! Ed Boele is famous for his wide selection of Dutch and foreign cheeses and has won several prices. Some cheeses are matured to perfection at a controlled temperature in a large display case in the back of the shop.

142 KROON KAASHANDEL

Van Hoytema-
straat 31
Haagse Hout ⑥
+31 (0)70 324 92 14
kroonkaas.nl

A tantalising shop for cheese lovers! The owner himself drives to the famous Rungis International Market in Paris to select the most delicious and rare cheeses. His beautiful tiny *chèvres* complete every cheese board. In addition to cheeses, Kroon also sells high-quality deli meats, like *Pata Negra* and *Bündnerfleisch*, among other delicacies.

143 KALKMAN

Frederik Hendrik-
laan 149
Scheveningen –
Statenkwartier ③
+31 (0)70 355 18 80
www.kalkmankaas.nl

Thanks to his wide choice of high-quality Dutch and foreign cheeses, Kalkman is a favourite cheesemonger in the expat neighbourhood Statenkwartier. The friendly staff is willing to let you taste before you buy. Besides cheese, Kalkman also sells very good home-roasted nuts. It's hard to leave this shop empty handed.

144 PROEFHUYS

Van Schagenstraat 11
Voorburg ⑦
+31 (0)70 387 24 58
proefhuys.nl

The owner, Jochem Beijer, is not only a cheesemonger but also an oenologist, a wine expert. In addition to a wide variety of Dutch and foreign cheeses, he sells great wines too. A real treat are the special (seasonal) cheeses like Vacherin, L'Etivaz and clothbound cheddar from Somerset. Jochem knows better than anyone how to pair wine and cheese.

145 ALEXANDERHOEVE DEN HAAG

Bankastraat 44
Archipel ④
+31 (0) 70 355 02 44
alexanderhoevekaas.nl

Annelies, the owner, is always willing to let you try one of the many cheeses in her shop. She has a huge variety of Dutch and foreign cheeses. She likes to pair cheese with beer, and sells several speciality beers as well. Together with the owners of the famous The Hague beer brand Kompaan she developed an appetising 'beer cheese'.

5 mouth-watering
DELIS

146 VERS UIT DE GERS

Kanaalweg 36
Scheveningen –
Visserijbuurt ⑤
+31 (0)6 50 24 01 01
versuitdegers.nl

In this narrow shop, once a shed where bicycles were stored, Ton and Veronica sell attractive strings of purple garlic and other French delicacies. The two import all the goodies from France themselves, since they have a second home in the Gers region. The garlic is very popular: they import and sell around 5000 kilos a year.

146 VERS UIT DE GERS

147 TRAITEUR LE GÔNE

Noordeinde 200-C
Hofkwartier ②
+31 (0)70 362 50 26
hetnoordeinde.nl/
horeca/le-gone_1

Get your French fix at this small traiteur/ eatery which serves and sells authentic food from mostly the Lyon region. The food, the ambiance, and even the staff are French. Sit down for lunch to have a *plat du jour* with a glass of red wine or just order a delicious sandwich to take away.

148 ELPIDIO

Herenstraat 114
Voorburg ⑦
+31 (0)70 322 00 87
elpidio.nl

This *enoteca*/deli in the historic heart of Voorburg is little Italy. The shop is filled to the brim with Italian delicacies. Drink a quick espresso, or sit down at one of the few tables and enjoy a small Italian dish or a sandwich with a good glass of wine.

149 GRANSJEAN

Bankastraat 12
Archipel ④
+31 (0)70 350 39 80
gransjean.nl

This shop has everything: wine, champagne, Dutch and foreign cheeses, chocolate, spices, olive oils, canned sardines, rare salts, and so on. Gransjean imports many delicacies direct from the source and sells local specialities, like honey by Haagse Honing, as well. A must for sophisticated gourmets.

150 MEZA

Frederik
Hendriklaan 115-A
Scheveningen –
Statenkwartier ③
+31 (0)70 324 78 71
meza.nl

The long counter with large platters of Lebanese food at this family-owned deli is very inviting. *Fattoush*, tabbouleh, aubergines with chickpeas or ground meat, *fatayer* (meat or cheese pie), and much more: everything is made fresh daily. You can either take the food out or have lunch at one of the few tables.

5 amazing places for
BREAD, PASTRY and PATISSERIE

---

151 LEKKER BROOD

Herengracht 16
Voorhout ②
+31 (0)70 363 66 17
lekkerbrood.nl

Situated in a beautifully tiled old delicatessen shop, Lekker Brood sells all sorts of organic bread: from multigrain and spelt bread to special bread varieties like *wakame* bread and red beet bread. At lunchtime people flock in for a freshly made sandwich.

152 BOULANGERIE MICHEL

2e Schuytstraat 121
Scheveningen –
Duinoord ③
+31 (0)70 737 08 63
boulangeriemichel.com

A good French bakery is a must in expat city The Hague. Boulangerie Michel has several locations around town. Some are bakery shops, others, like the one in 2e Schuytstraat, are breakfast and lunch cafes as well. The crusty baguettes and the buttery croissants are among the best in the city.

153 DS PATISSERIE

Denneweg 136
Voorhout ②
+31 (0)6 14 34 15 05
dspatisserie.nl

Owner Kelly Koopmans is very skilled and thus creates the most exquisite French delicacies, such as macarons, éclairs and *tartelettes*. However, it is not only French patisserie she is good at. When the Dutch celebrate Saint Nicholas in December, she makes delicious Dutch goodies, like chocolate letters, marzipan and *speculaas*.

154 PHILIPPE GALERNE

Aert van der
Goesstraat 24
Scheveningen –
Statenkwartier ③
+31 (0)70 338 86 62
philippegalerne.nl

Since its opening in 2006, this French patisserie in the international Statenkwartier is very popular among expats and locals alike. On weekends, people queue here for fresh croissants and baguettes. Galerne is also renowned for his patisserie, that he makes with fresh seasonal ingredients.

155 TARTINE

Van Beverningk-
straat 101
Scheveningen –
Statenkwartier ③
+31 (0)70 406 22 78
tartinedenhaag.nl

Early 2022, in a former garage, Denis Botrot opened his dream shop, a French patisserie. His handmade pies, éclairs and madeleines are dangerously delicious. Besides patisserie he also offers several savoury dishes, such as smoked salmon salad, rillette and homemade Dutch *bitterballen* with a French twist.

152 BOULANGERIE MICHEL

5 great shops to buy
TEA OR COFFEE

156 **INPROC**

Denneweg 63
Voorhout ②
+31 (0)70 346 15 41
inproc.nl

Cosy, casual and around since 1853, when the shop started selling products imported from the Dutch East Indies. As of 2015, this beloved and timeless tea and coffee shop is run by Krista Buys. She roasts the coffee beans herself and creates the most wonderful coffee and tea blends. The Melati, a mix of eight different teas, has been popular for years.

157 BOON

157 BOON

Prinsestraat 114
Hofkwartier ②
+31 (0)70 744 49 72
koffiebranderijboon.nl

When Lianne starts roasting, just follow your nose and you will find this charming place! At this coffee bar and roastery, you can buy speciality coffees roasted by the owner herself. Customers can also drink an espresso, cappuccino or latte at the two tables inside or at the tiny terrace on the pavement. Just coffee, no food.

158 KALI TENGAH

Weimarstraat 54
Segbroek ⑧
+31 (0)70 744 68 69
kalitengah.nl

Looking for a special kind of loose tea? Go to Kali Tengah. This shop has an outstanding (organic) tea selection. In addition to tea, it sells several speciality coffee brands like the local BOON. It also carries tea and coffee accessories such as the lovely Bredemeijer teapots.

159 ESPRESSO PERFETTO

Prinsestraat 47
Hofkwartier ②
+31 (0)70 360 10 41
espressoperfetto-denhaag.nl

The core business of this tiny coffee bar is the sale and repair of quality espresso machines. Espresso Perfetto has various small models on display, like Vibiemme, BFC, Isomac and Pavoni. Besides coffee machines you can also find your favourite brand of coffee here.

160 LENTE THEE EN CHOCOLADE

Marcelisstraat 255-B
Scheveningen –
Visserijbuurt ⑤
+31 (0)70 752 20 94
lentetheechocolade.nl

Marjolein Ham, the owner of this cute shop, regularly travels to Darjeeling in India to pick the best tea leaves for her teas. She is very passionate about quality and sells beautiful teas from mostly India, Nepal and Japan. Besides tea you can also get high-quality chocolate and honey from The Hague here.

5 indispensable shops to buy
CHOCOLATE

---

161 HOP & STORK

AT: DE PASSAGE
SHOPPING CENTRE
Passage 82
Old Centre ①
+31 (0)70 345 54 55
hopandstork.com

It's impossible to leave this chocolatier in De Passage without a chocolate treat. At the counter bonbons, truffles and thick chunks of tantalising chocolate are attractively displayed. In their adjacent coffee room, you can enjoy an outstanding cup of coffee and a sweet seasonal pastry. In summer, Hop & Stork offers high-quality ice cream as well.

162 BONBON-ATELIER WESTERBEEK

Van Slingelandt-
straat 121
Scheveningen –
Statenkwartier ③
+31 (0)70 350 78 21
bonbonatelier
westerbeek.nl

This shop comes with an incredible story. Owner Nico Fernandes inherited the shop some 25 years ago from Guus Westerbeek, a renowned chocolatier in his day. Fernandes was flabbergasted as he had met the chocolatier only once. He decided to take the chance and submerged himself in the art of chocolate making. With success. This is still one of the best places in town for handmade bonbons.

163 THE CHOCOLATE-SHOP

Limoenhof 1
Segbroek ⑧
+31 (0)6 14 85 45 42
thechocolateshop.nl

Chocolate lovers know to find this cute hip shop despite its location in a residential area. The owners, Sanna and Ray, are always in search for the best and most sustainable bean-to-bar chocolate. Enjoy their chocolate with a sublime cup of coffee on the spot or book one of their interesting chocolate workshops.

164 DE BONTE KOE

Korte Poten 57
Uilebomen ②
debontekoe.nl

You will always find people looking in awe at the giant chocolate cow's head in the shop window. It's a funny reference to the name of the shop, 'the spotted cow', and to the fact that in the old days the place used to be a butcher's. This chocolatier sells delicious bonbons and tasty bars. The 'Haagsche Hopjes' bars, named after the famous coffee caramels, are a great souvenir.

165 PÂTISSERIE CHOCOLATERIE JARREAU

Van Hoytema-
straat 42
Haagse Hout ⑥
+31 (0)70 324 87 19
jarreau.nl

People with sweet tooth will not be disappointed at Jarreau. Located in a chic neighbourhood not far from where the royal family lives, this is one of the fanciest patisseries and chocolatiers in town. In addition to the finest *petit fours,* macarons and cakes, Jarreau creates the most beautiful and delectable bonbons. Try the famous Goldrush bonbon, a prizewinner.

The 5 best
NON-WESTERN FOOD
shops

---

166 MARAKESH

Stationsweg 134
Stationsbuurt ①
+31 (0)70 380 22 41
marakesh.nl

The enormous piles of beautifully shaped Moroccan cookies at this Moroccan bakery are simply irresistible. Deep fried *chebakia, briwats* filled with almond paste, aniseed cookies, date cookies, and many more traditional Moroccan sweet treats can be found here.

167 INDIA GATE

Hobbemaplein 50
Schilderswijk ⑨
+31 (0)70 356 30 62
india-gate.nl

Here is a must-go place for foodies. All the Indian spices and ingredients you can dream of are available at this shop. From large bags of basmati rice, lentils, *chapatti* flour and chickpea flour to spice mixes, fresh Indian vegetables, and even Indian *barfi* (sweets).

168 SURINAAMSE MARKT

De Heemstraat 166
Schilderswijk ⑨

Upon entering this shop, you suddenly find yourself in Surinam. Stacks of *koepila* (smoked and dried catfish), large bundles of *yardlong* beans, piles of *okra*, colourful Madame Jeanette peppers, *tayer*, and more, fill the shelves. The friendly staff are willing to help you pick the best masala, or to explain how to make authentic *pom*, a festive Surinam dish.

169 AMAZING ORIENTAL YPENBURG

Laan van
Haamstede 36
Leidschenveen-
Ypenburg ⑦
+31 (0)70 762 28 88
amazingoriental.com

The biggest Asian supermarket of
The Hague, and maybe the Netherlands!
If you are looking for specific Chinese,
Japanese, Korean, or Vietnamese
ingredients, this is your place. You
will find a huge variety of fresh Asian
vegetables, a fresh fish department,
a great selection of Asian kitchenware,
and even a restaurant here.

170 RN PRODUCTOS LATINOS

Van Swinden-
straat 118
Segbroek ⑧
+31 (0)6 47 86 74 19
rn-productoslatinos.nl

The owners, Richard and his Colombian
wife Patricia, import products from
many Latin American countries, which
they sell in their clean little shop.
They also serve Colombian coffee, hot
chocolate and tropical fruit shakes, plus
Colombian snacks. On Sundays it can get
crowded, when people meet here after
the Spanish mass.

168 SURINAAMSE MARKT

5 special
WINE BOUTIQUES

171 VINO VERO

Weimarstraat 36
Segbroek ⑧
+31 (0)70 302 02 00
vinovero.nl

Vino Vero is specialised in organic wines. The friendly owners of this cute wine shop are always willing to let you taste their beautiful wines. On Saturdays, at the end of the day, it can be crowded here with customers and friends passing by for a sip and a bottle. Only open on Thursday, Friday and Saturday.

172 DE FILOSOOF

Papestraat 5
Hofkwartier ②
+31 (0)70 230 06 02
de-filosoof.nl

Socrates, the gorgeous Persian cat, will welcome you to this tiny shop, which is also a place where philosophers, authors and poets meet. The competent owner, a philosopher and poet himself, is originally from Afghanistan. He imports exclusive wines, also from lesser known places such as Azerbaijan. He also distils and sells his own excellent gin, called... Socrates.

173 MARIUS JOUW WIJNVRIEND!

Piet Heinstraat 93
Zeeheldenkwartier ④
+31 (0)70 363 31 00
jouwwijnvriend.nl

Marius is every wine lover's friend! From the bottom to the top this delightful shop is filled with the best bottles of wine for all budgets. The shop delivers wine to many hip eateries in town, from bistros to upscale restaurants. You can book a wine tasting with food in the adjacent room.

174 WIJNHANDEL KOOPER

Prins Hendrik-
straat 43-A
Zeeheldenkwartier ③
+31 (0)70 363 70 16

This pleasantly old-fashioned shop with a jovial owner has been around for decades. And it has much more to offer than wine alone. Kooper has amazing and exclusive collections of Kopke Port (very old and rare bottles can be purchased here), grappa, malt whisky, eau de vie, and Dutch Van Wees genever and liquor.

175 HET HAAGS WIJNHUIS (PAVIE WINES & GIFTS)

Reinkenstraat 13
Scheveningen –
Duinoord ③
+31 (0)70 356 08 05
pavie.nl

It is said that the French ambassador purchases wines at this wine shop specialised in bottles from the Burgundy and Bordeaux regions. And that's saying something. Because of the close collaboration with a wine auction in Antwerp, this shop regularly has new treasures in stock. From very exclusive old wines to affordable bottles, Het Haags Wijnhuis has it all.

The 5 best
SPECIALITY SHOPS

---

176 DROGISTERIJ VAN DER GAAG

Dagelijkse Groen-
markt 27
Old Centre ①
+31 (0)70 346 24 13
*drogisterij
vandergaag.nl*

This chemist's shop dating back to 1769 breathes history. The large yawning head above the entrance (an old Dutch sign for a chemist), old pharmacy wooden drawers, barrels, bottles, scales: it's one of the best-preserved old shops in town. However, the products this chemist's shop sells are very up to date.

177 FREE BEER CO.

177 FREE BEER CO.

Prinsestraat 59
Hofkwartier ②
+31 (0)70 331 13 92

The Canadian owner missed the kind of hip beer shop that is prevalent in Canada, so he opened Free Beer Company. At his teeny-weeny shop with laidback vibes, he offers three exclusive beers on tap. Since this is not a bar, you take the beer home with you in large jugs.

178 GOEDMAN ART SUPPLIES

Prins Hendrik-
straat 51
Zeeheldenkwartier ③
+31 (0)70 345 13 24
rolfgoedman.nl

In a city where the Royal Academy of Art is located, a shop with high-quality art supplies is a must. Goedman, with more than 100 years of experience, has it all. Everything you need for painting, drawing, block printing, calligraphy, and more, can be found here. Goedman also has a picture frame studio next door.

179 WEMPE & WEMPE

Buitenom 4
Old Centre ①
+31 (0)70 388 94 98
wempewempe.nl

Off the beaten path, open since 1989, and still going strong. In chic The Hague, where private dinner parties at home are commonplace, people know to find this delightful shop for antique and vintage china. You just might find that missing Villeroy & Boch plate or Wedgwood saucer here.

180 HOUSE OF HATS

Papestraat 24
Hofkwartier ②
+31 (0)70 406 00 53
houseofhats.nl

'For everyone a hat and cap!', that is Susan Dekker's motto. At her adorable shop, you'll find hats that can be worn every day: renowned and stylish brands like Stetson and Borsalino, but also lesser known brands like ReHats, cool upcycled hats made of used coffee bean sacks.

5 *great*
VINTAGE & RETRO INTERIOR SHOPS

---

181 OLD PINE SHOP

Suezkade 48
Segbroek ⑧
+31 (0)6 55 90 03 45
littlegreen-shop.nl

If you want to give your home a facelift in a sustainable way, go to this beautiful shop at the Suezkade. The owner Zoë is super creative and always willing to help you with some great styling ideas. She sells secondhand ceramics, rare objects, small furniture, dried flowers, plants, and more. She also collaborates with local artists. A must-visit!

182 SPRINKEL + HOP

Weimarstraat 19
Segbroek ⑧
+31 (0)6 47 96 43 26
sprinkelhop.nl

Walking into this cute shop feels like stepping into a retro living room, decorated with items from especially the fifties and sixties. Think brass bar carts and side tables, glass and Formica coffee tables, rotan chairs and magazine racks. The shop also has a great collection of lamps, coloured glassware, vintage flower vases and mirrors.

181 **OLD PINE SHOP**

183 PRESENT LIVING

Piet Heinstraat 99
Zeeheldenkwartier ④
+31 (0)6 48 51 72 28
presentliving.nl

The owner often travels to France and England in search of *brocantes*. He comes back with old closets, mirrors, tables, suitcases, kitchenware, piles of gorgeous, decorated plates, and more. Most of the furniture gets a white paint job before being displayed, which brings harmony to the shop. You'll also find a few contemporary items here, such as plants, bags and jewellery.

184 BENNIES FIFTIES

Namensestraat 73
Scheveningen –
Belgisch Park ⑤
+31 (0)70 358 58 10
fiftiesstore.com

If you are mad about the American fifties, this is your place. The owners regularly travel to the US to load a container with vintage jukeboxes, pinball machines, neon signs, street signs, license plates, diner furniture, original gas pumps, and much more. Besides vintage stuff, Bennies sells new retro items as well.

185 DEJA VINTAGE

Westvlietweg 74
Leidschenveen-
Ypenburg ⑦
+31 (0)6 23 44 34 53
dejavintage.com

Mid-century furniture is hip and happening again and Deja Vintage has one of the largest collections in town. In the storage space on the edge of The Hague, you will find teak sideboards, leather sofas, brass serving trolleys, nesting tables, and more. The furniture is in good condition and many of the items are by well-known designers.

The 5 best
LIFESTYLE & CONCEPT STORES

---

186 POUSH.

Frederik Hendrik-
laan 245
Scheveningen –
Statenkwartier ③
+31 (0)6 15 38 73 25
poush.nl

This is a shop-in-shop place where small, mostly Dutch, businesses can sell their unique products. Think affordable jewellery, fashion, bags, scarfs, stationary and small home decoration items. Every product tells a story. Great place if you are looking for a present.

187 STIJLBANDIET

Fahrenheitstraat 644
Segbroek ⑧
stijlbandiet.nl

Trendy women's clothing and accessories, cute baby stuff, cool gifts, beautiful tableware and home decoration items. This large, attractive lifestyle store in the Fahrenheitstraat, run by mother and daughter, is a true gem. Here you'll find fashion brands like MSCH, Lois Jeans, ESTHRZ and VILA.

188 COUQOU

Noordeinde 59
Hofkwartier ②
+31 (0)6 14 03 52 03
couqou.com

Tucked away in an alley at Noordeinde, you'll find Couqou, a creative shop run by a young couple. Niek designs the cool modern furniture, Jacqueline the lamp shades, and her father the leather bags. All this combined with some basic clothes, jewellery and home decoration items.

189 PR8T1G

Herenstraat 81
Voorburg ⑦
+31 (0)6 24 26 13 22
PR8T1G.nl

The name of this little lifestyle shop is pronounced as *prachtig*, gorgeous in English. Located at the historic heart of Voorburg, this really is a delightful spot. The owner Vivien de Bruijn sells what she's passionate about, like Bufandy scarfs, Yeez Louise shirts (YZLS), MIAB jewels. But the most beautiful items might be the sturdy leather bags, designed by herself!

190 DE HUISHOUD-WINKEL

Piet Heinstraat 102
Zeeheldenkwartier ③
dehuishoudwinkel.nl

At this 'Household Shop' the focus lies on sustainable cleaning products and tools. No plastic brooms and buckets here, but sturdy wooden and iron household supplies. They also sell sustainable beauty products and hip home decoration items, like ceramics, linen napkins and ecofriendly candles.

190 DE HUISHOUDWINKEL

The 5 best
FURNITURE & HOME
DECORATION *shops*

191 WATT DESIGN

Laan van
Meerdervoort 94-A
Zeeheldenkwartier ③
+31 (0)70 363 06 01
wattdesign.nl

Looking for a special lamp or sofa to perk up your home? Visit the spacious and beautiful shop on Laan van Meerdervoort and marvel at the designer lamps and furniture. This lighting and furniture shop has been around for more than 30 years. It is specialised in art deco and modern design and carries many Dutch designer brands.

192 LASAS & LOEKOV

Grote Markt-
straat 16-A
Old Centre ①
+31 (0)70 205 56 36
lasasenloekov.nl

You wouldn't expect such a warm and personal interior decoration shop sitting at the largest shopping street of The Hague. Its collection is a nice combination of trendy furniture, lamps, rugs and decoration items. Next to the shop, the owners opened a kiosk where you can get freshly made Dutch *poffertjes* and good barista coffee. If you buy a piece of furniture the treat is on the house.

193 MAS

Frederikstraat 565
Willemspark ④
+31 (0)70 345 09 03
masinterieur.nl

MAS interior design is synonymous with cool modern home decor. The large showroom – with furniture, lighting, rugs and the most beautiful fabrics by upscale designer brands – is very inspirational. MAS is not guided by trends: the modern designs are fresh and often timeless. MAS also provides a complete interior design service, should you need one.

194 STUDIO VAN 'T WOUT

Zeestraat 94
Zeeheldenkwartier ④
+31 (0)70 392 27 47
studiovantwout.nl

The owners of this large interior design shop actually live in the shop: their marvellous home on the first floor is part of the showroom. What a brilliant idea! Here you'll find the best inspiration for your new interior. The style of Studio van 't Wout is not based on trends but modern, timeless and luxurious instead.

195 EDWIN PELSER

Piet Heinstraat 123
Zeeheldenkwartier ④
+31 (0)70 360 92 37
edwinpelser.nl

Here you'll experience that modern design can be intimate and personal. The owner of this furniture and home decoration shop, Edwin Pelser, only sells pieces by Dutch and international designers he believes in. Designers who each tell a unique story. Flagship brands are the Danish Muuto and the Dutch label Vij5. Do visit the little garden with eye-catching Dutch Weltevree furniture!

193 MAS

The 5 best
GIFT SHOPS

196 WAUW

Piet Heinstraat 51-A
Zeeheldenkwartier ④
+31 (0)70 201 37 37
wauwwarenhuis.nl

The interior of this little gift shop with plants, vintage furniture and curiosities is worth a visit in itself. Further, WAUW sells presents you won't find easily elsewhere, like handmade jewellery, beautiful stationary and home decoration items.

197 WNKL

Piet Heinstraat 57
Zeeheldenkwartier ④
+31 (0)70 887 62 36
wnkldenhaag.nl

The perfect giftshop for the conscious giver with an eye for detail and design. At WNKL you'll find beautiful printed textiles, handmade leather bags and wallets, original lamps, toys, vases, soaps, stationary and much more. All the brands have a unique story. It's hard to leave empty-handed.

198 THE HAGUE'S FINEST

Venestraat 20
Old Centre ①
+31 (0)70 820 99 46
thehaguesfinest.com

The best souvenirs are the ones that are sustainably and locally crafted. And wow, on that front The Hague has a lot to offer! This big, bright store in the centre of town is stocked with locally produced food and beverages (like sausages, chocolate, beer and gin), home decoration and garden items, music, art, beauty products, clothes, and much more.

199 HET APPELTAART-GEVOEL

Noordeinde 79
Hofkwartier ②
+31 (0)70 737 02 17
hetappeltaartgevoel.nl

Is there anyone who doesn't like apple pie? This shop wants to give you that warm, cosy and delicious 'apple pie feeling' (*appeltaartgevoel*). With success, for it sells all you need to create the right ambiance: from lovely presents to small interior and stationery items. In summer, you can have a piece of apple pie in the garden behind the shop.

200 WAAR

Fahrenheitstraat 496
Segbroek ⑧
+31 (0)70 205 02 68
ditiswaar.nl

Ethical and sustainable gifts! Fashion, home decoration items, food and books: everything is organic, recycled, fair trade, and environmentally friendly. Beautiful, trendy items for people who care for themselves, others and the earth. Even the shop is constructed and decorated with sustainable materials.

198 THE HAGUE'S FINEST

The 5 most inspiring
JEWELLERY SHOPS

201 LIESBETH BUSMAN
Prinsegracht 32
Old Centre ①
+31 (0)70 889 16 30
liesbethbusman.nl

The energetic goldsmith Liesbeth Busman gets her inspiration from nature. Coral, twigs, wings, but also the vast landscape of the Kalahari Desert are reflected in her precious jewellery. She works with recycled silver and gold and uses conflict-free gemstones. Her impressive atelier in a historical building downtown makes a visit extra special.

201 LIESBETH BUSMAN

202 LAURIE HERMELER

Oude Molstraat 7
Hofkwartier ②
+31 (0)70 331 15 59
lauriehermeler.nl

If you are looking for a beautiful one-off piece, Laurie Hermeler might be your goldsmith. At her cosy atelier/shop, she designs the most wonderful rings, earrings and necklaces. She loves to turn old jewellery into something precious and new, and often works with unique gemstones.

203 GALERIE GUTHSCHMIDT

Prinsestraat 39-43
Hofkwartier ②
+31 (0)6 12 46 85 27
galerieguthschmidt.nl

This gallery for contemporary jewellery and objects has about 30 Dutch and international designers on display, unique designers that use various techniques and materials. It offers for example gorgeous pieces in gold or silver by Ria Lins or Nicolette van Hattum.

204 PEPITA D'ORO

Thomsonlaan 104-A
Segbroek ⑧
+31 (0)70 330 66 40
pepitadoro.nl

In her studio/shop the talented and young goldsmith Rose creates wearable and trendy rings, necklaces, bracelets and earrings. Many of the tools she uses, she inherited from her grandmother, who also was a goldsmith. Available in her bright little shop are her own label Charlierose, as well as some other affordable brands.

205 OH DEAR

Molenstraat 56
Hofkwartier ②
+31 (0)70 870 06 07
ohdearshop.com

Four jewellery designers under one roof. At this original studio/shop you can often see the goldsmiths at work. The four designers each have different styles, but they all turn gold, silver and gemstones into precious jewellery.

5 great shops to buy
VINTAGE &
SECONDHAND
CLOTHING

206 SPOOKY & SUE

Conradkade 34
Segbroek ⑧
+31 (0)6 19 98 77 15
spookyandsue.nl

Give clothes, shoes and bags a second life! SPOOKY & SUE sells stylish vintage and secondhand stuff in very good condition and for reasonable prices. You'll find quality brands here, like Claudia Sträter, KOOKAÏ, King Louie, you name it.

207 ZUSJES VINTAGE BOETIEK

Boekhorststraat 93
Old Centre ①
zusjesvintageboetiek.
business.site

The two owners of this vintage shop, Sanne and Moniek, source the clothes themselves and look for unique pieces from the last century. Clothes that are classic in style but still relevant today. All the items are clean and ironed. The art-nouveau shop is spacious, well organised and just beautiful. A must!

208 ILKA VINTAGE

Sumatrastraat 160
Archipel ④
+31 (0)6 14 61 44 08
ilkavintage.nl

Head to this intimate boutique with quality vintage and secondhand clothing if you want to treat yourself without guilt to (designer) items. At Ilka Vintage, you'll find affordable and hidden gems, like a summer dress by La Fée Maraboutée or a stunning pair of Prada shoes.

209 APPEL & EI
Papestraat 17
Hofkwartier ②
+31 (0)70 206 00 20
appelenei.nl

You will hardly notice that this is a vintage store. The secondhand clothing is in mint condition, smells fresh, and is never more than three seasons old. Appel & Ei also sells 'leftover' new items. This large, bright store is a must-visit for anyone who cares for the planet.

210 EVY'S
Prinses Marie-
straat 7-C
Willemspark ④
+31 (0)6 27 31 08 43
evysvintage.nl

Upmarket brand clothing in mint condition, that's what you get at this little romantic vintage shop. A Tomas Maier dress, a pair of Gucci shoes, a Prada bag, or Chanel earrings, every item is carefully picked by the owner.

207 ZUSJES VINTAGE BOETIEK

The 5 best
FASHION BOUTIQUES
FOR HER

---

211 VANPEET

Frederikstraat 78
Willemspark ④
+31 (0)70 345 55 05

Fashion for elegant women with guts, this is the motto of this attractive small boutique. The shop is very well-stocked, so it's hard to leave empty handed. You'll find fashionable dresses, coats, skirts, scarfs and belts, but also cool leather trousers and jackets.

214 JUST

212 WWEN

Prinsestraat 70
Hofkwartier ②
+31 (0)70 392 77 73
wwen.nl

The collection of WWen is not only colorful, creative and unique, but also sustainable. Many items are made with environmentally friendly materials like bamboo, organic cotton and hemp. At this cute shop you'll find a large range of organic and fair trade brands.

213 OWN & CLUB

Denneweg 114-C
Voorhout ②
+31 (0)70 345 03 33
own-club.nl

This spacious and inviting shop carries many hip Dutch and international clothing labels. There is something for every taste, like basic comfortable knitwear by American Vintage, cheerful dresses by Freebird, or bold leather jackets by Goosecraft.

214 JUST

Molenstraat 43
Hofkwartier ②
+31 (0)70 200 26 66
just-denhaag.nl

Don't just walk by this teeny-weeny boutique in one of the most picturesque streets of the city! At Just you'll find hip and affordable (Dutch) clothing and accessories brands, like Zusss, Birds on the Run and A Beautiful Story. There is a secondhand clothes section in the back.

215 ART & CASEY

Korte Poten 36
Uilebomen ②
+31 (0)70 360 97 49
artencasey.nl

This fashion boutique offers a nice mix of sustainable and (smaller) designer brands. Cheerful labels like Avoca, Happy Rainy Days, La Fée Maraboutée, Nathalie Vleeschouwer, People Tree and See U Soon, as well as retro and vintage items can be found here. They also sell some shoes and bags.

The 5 best
FASHION BOUTIQUES FOR HIM

---

216 **STORE DU NORD**
Noordeinde 49
Hofkwartier ②
+31 (0)70 737 02 34
storedunord.com

The well-being of our planet is a high priority at Store Du Nord. The owner really puts an effort into finding well-made garments by independent designers and small-scale manufacturers who share his vision. The result is a beautiful boutique where you can find unique items. Slow fashion at its best!

217 **ETTEMADIS**
Noordeinde 88
Hofkwartier ②
+31 (0)70 215 62 05
ettemadis.com

Although the roots of this Hague tailor date back to the fifties in Tehran, it tailors to the classy, modern man. Everything – from smart casual, shirts and ties to business suits – is designed according to the latest trends and handmade at its beautiful Noordeinde premises. How much more 'Haags' does it get?

218 **UPTOWN**

Prinsestraat 2-C
Hofkwartier ②
+31 (0)70 412 94 04
uptown-denhaag.nl

Just outside the main shopping area you'll find the upscale boutiques, like Uptown. This large men's fashion shop for the young and trendy has brands like Won Hundred, Maison Kitsuné, Stüssy, AMI Paris, Jason Markk and Libertine-Libertine. The splendid interior of this place adds to the shopping experience.

219 **WHITE**

Denneweg 116
Voorhout ②
+31 (0)70 756 04 93
whiteonline.nl

Fashion-conscious men love this place! The ambience is very man-friendly, with dark colours, a vintage motorcycle, and several places to sit. On weekends, there is wine, cheese, whisky, and a team of goodlooking salesmen to help you make the right decisions. White sells classy and sturdy clothes by high-quality and unique brands.

220 **BENDORFF**

Prinsestraat 11
Hofkwartier ②
+31 (0)70 364 41 14

A large and well-organised shop with casual clothing and accessories for men. It carries brands like J.Lindeberg, RVLT Revolution and the affordable Dstrezzed. Bendorff specialises in denim and has cool jeans by Diesel, Kings of Indigo and Nudie. Do not miss the vinyl records corner!

5 places to buy special
SHOES

―――――――――

221 BOOTS BY M

Noordeinde 100
Hofkwartier ②
+31 (0)70 346 39 55
bootsbym.nl

Every fashion-conscious person needs a striking pair of handmade western or cowboy boots in her or his closet! Boots by M sells the genuine stuff, such as Lucchese, the top-quality brand from Texas and worn by many celebs, and the richly decorated Old Gringo boots. Besides boots, this shop also offers leather belts, beautiful bags and purses, and many other accessories.

222 REINHARD FRANS

Frederikstraat 8
Willemspark ④
+31 (0)70 427 58 75
reinhardfrans.nl

The motto of this Dutch family-run business is 'affordable luxury'. And they succeed, for at this shop you can buy handcrafted men's shoes for a very reasonable price. The elegant shoes are made with high-quality calf-skin leather and are coloured by hand. Every pair is unique.

223 NICONICO

Frederikstraat 45
Willemspark ④
+31 (0)70 360 42 08
niconico.nl

Some 20 years ago, this store started out as a children's shoe store. Today, owner Nicole sells mainly women's shoes and clothes, but you can still get some good-quality children's shoes here too. You'll find smaller exclusive brands from Scandinavian, Italian and French designers.

224 DE RODE LOPER

Hoogstraat 26
Hofkwartier ②
+31 (0)70 365 02 55
derodeloper.nl

Not exactly a place for the faint of heart; the shoes with bold and extravagant designs are sold to proud cosmopolitan wearers, who care for luxury and detail. Gucci, Givenchy, Saint Laurent, Balenciaga, Isabel Marant, all the high-end international brands can be purchased here. For glamorous women and men.

225 HUYKMAN & DUYVESTEIN

Zilverstraat 21
Escamp ⑨
+31 (70) 366 18 98
hdos.nl

Shoemakers since 1781, this family-run business has over the centuries kept up with the times. Here, men go for trendy, self-designed shoes crafted by hand. The finest leather is used, and shoes come in various sparkling colours. This is not a shop, but a workplace with a showroom.

The 5 best
BOOKSHOPS

226 DOUWES

Herengracht 60
Old Centre ②
+31 (0)70 737 11 26
boekhandeldouwes.nl

This bookshop recently took over the fabulous collection of the Stanley & Livingstone travel bookshop and now has the largest travel collection of The Hague. Globes, world maps, hiking and cycling maps are also sold here. Besides travel books, they are specialised in trains and railways and legal books. Their general collection won't disappoint either.

227 PAAGMAN

Frederik Hendrik-
laan 217
Scheveningen –
Statenkwartier ③
+31 (0)88 338 38 38
paagman.nl

There is always something going on at this large family-owned bookshop: book signings, performances, small events. You can easily spend hours here, for this bookshop also has a cosy cafe. Located in the neighbourhood where many expats live, Paagman sells English books as well.

228 **PARIMAR BOEKEN**

Korte Molen-
straat 17-A
Hofkwartier ②
+31 (0)70 365 82 26
parimar.nl

This is the go-to bookshop for remainder books. The owner of this adorable shop buys books from mostly American and English publishing houses and sells them for half of the original price. Think beautiful coffee-table art and photography books, but also cookbooks, history books, travel guides, literature and lovely (pop-up) children's books.

229 **DE VRIES VAN STOCKUM**

Passage 11
Old Centre ①
+31 (0)70 302 81 10
devriesvanstockum.nl

Bookshops are having a hard time. Nowadays, to attract customers, a bookshop must be extra inviting, appealing, and special. De Vries Van Stockum has it all. With its super central location in the elegant Passage, it could not have been better. The staff are knowledgeable and they have English books as well.

230 **ABC (AMERICAN BOOK CENTER)**

Lange Poten 23
Uilebomen ②
+31 (0)70 364 27 42
abc.nl

The ultimate bookshop for English-speaking expats in The Hague! ABC, a family-owned bookshop, has a wide selection of English books, both fiction and non-fiction. And if you happen to miss your favourite American magazines, this is also your place. Do not forget to take a look at the secondhand books section on the first floor.

The 5 most inspiring
ART GALLERIES *and*
ART RENTALS

---

231 HEDEN
Denneweg 14-A
Voorhout ②
+31 (0)70 346 53 37
heden.nl

At Heden on the Denneweg, you can lease or buy art, or just walk in to visit one of the free exhibitions. It also offers a platform for beginning and talented artists and organises events on a regularly basis. One of the primary goals of Heden is to make art accessible to everyone.

232 HAAGSE KUNSTKRING
Denneweg 64
Voorhout ②
+31 (0)70 364 75 85
haagsekunstkring.nl

This art society has been around since 1891. The membership list with many well-known artists, writers, architects, musicians and photographers is impressive. The society organises expositions, readings, concerts, workshops and dinner parties.

233 DE GALERIE DEN HAAG
Noordeinde 69-71
Hofkwartier ②
+31 (0)70 392 08 13
degaleriedenhaag.nl

Coen van den Oever is the owner of two adjacent contemporary art galleries at Noordeinde: De Galerie and Project 2.0./ Gallery (Noordeinde 57), also an art rental. You can rent or buy etchings, lithographs, silk screens, photographs and original paintings here. Project 2.0 focusses on edgy art by renowned Dutch and international artists.

234 GALERIE RAMAKERS

Toussaintkade 51
Zeeheldenkwartier ④
+31 (0)70 363 43 08
galerieramakers.nl

This gallery, which has been around since 1994, delivers serious, edgy exhibitions. The founder, Catalijn Ramakers, wanted a place where she could show what she was interested in: foremost experimental, contemporary minimalist and surreal art. Dutch and international renowned artists like Pat Andrea, Klaus Baumgärtner, Ossip and Warffemius are shown here.

235 DÜRST BRITT & MAYHEW

Van Limburg
Stirumstraat 47
Stationsbuurt ①
+31 (0)70 444 36 39
durstbrittmayhew.com

Hidden in a former garage near train station Hollands Spoor. The location of this cutting-edge gallery for contemporary art might not be an obvious one, but all art collectors know to find it. This gallery exhibits work by experimental Dutch and international artists.

231 HEDEN

The 5 best
SURF & SKATE
shops

---

236 NOORDZEE BOARDSTORE

Badhuisstraat 72
Scheveningen –
Visserijbuurt ⑤
+31 (0)70 201 51 53
noordzeeboardstore.nl

A surfer's paradise. This shop has everything you need for the ultimate surf experience: more than 175 surfboards in store (new and secondhand), wetsuits, accessories, and staff with a lot of know-how. Noordzee Boardstore also does board reparations.

236 NOORDZEE BOARDSTORE

237 ALOHA

Strand Noord 2-B
Scheveningen –
Beach ⑤
+31 (0)70 322 71 71
alohasurf.nl

A surf shop on the beach! Wetsuits, boards and surfing apparel: all the large brands can be purchased here. Besides a shop, Aloha is also a surf school and a beach pavilion with laidback vibes.

238 SHAKA

Vissershavenweg 62
Scheveningen –
Harbour ⑤
+31 (0)70 358 48 00
shakaonline.nl

Shaka Kitesurfing is both a shop and a kitesurfing school. The long coastline of The Hague with its sandy beaches and often a side-shore wind is great for kitesurfing. At this cosy shop you'll find all the gear you need, even complete kitesurfing sets and nice beachwear.

239 MANUS SKATESHOP

Papestraat 19
Hofkwartier ②
+31 (0)70 363 46 44

The owner of this small shop in the centre of town is very passionate when it comes to good-quality skateboards, shoes and clothing. He only sells the best of the best and supports small independent brands. A small shop, with high-quality items at competitive prices.

240 SICKBOARDS

Maanweg 24
Laak ⑦
+31 (0)70 870 05 01
sickboards.nl

Where to start at this huge and impressive shop with a large collection of longboards, street skateboards, streetwear and skate shoes? Luckily the friendly and knowledgeable staff are here to help you out. With an integrated skatepark, where you can actually try the boards before you buy them, this place is heaven for skateboarders.

5
LOCAL DESIGNERS
to check out

241 MOOFERS' SALON

Toussaintkade 22
Zeeheldenkwartier ④
+31 (0)70 205 74 84
moofersclothing.nl

Jennifer van Haastert founded Moofers Clothing, her women's fashion label, in 2017. Characteristic for her style is the use of sustainable fabrics and a sober but feminine and bold design with a timeless look and feel. At her new shop at the Toussaintkade she collaborates with a divers set of painters and artists.

242 MICHAEL BARNAART

Papestraat 1-B
Hofkwartier ②
+31 (0)70 744 57 05
michaelbarnaart.com

Fashion designer Michael Barnaart is famous for his tricot dresses. Comfortable dresses with modern and often fun prints. Well known is his black-blue-red Mondrian dress, but other dresses with printed belts, buttons and flowers are also characteristic.

243 BERRY RUTJES

Noordeinde 182
Hofkwartier ②
+31 (0)6 22 60 06 65
berryrutjes.com

In The Hague, design hats never go out of fashion. Berry Rutjes, the most famous local hat designer, designs hats for no one less than Queen Máxima. But also ordinary customers are welcome in her 'Salon Royal' at Noordeinde, which is open by appointment only. Better than anyone she knows which hat suits your face best.

244 STUDIO MRS. ROSEHIP

Stevinstraat 141
Scheveningen –
Belgisch Park ⑤
+31 (0)6 11 31 57 54
mrsrosehip.com
cursustassenmaken.nl

Bags by Mrs. Rosehip are instantly recognisable, for they are made of pleated leather, a labour-intensive process. The bags are chic, luxurious, sustainably made and can be purchased online or at Hotel des Indes; Mrs. Rosehip doesn't have a shop. Designer Roos van Put also has a private school for leather-bagmaking, where you can learn how to make your own Mrs. Rosehip bag.

245 SECRID

+31 (0)70 390 21 80
secrid.com

René and Marianne van Geer, the designers of the now world-famous card protector wallets Secrid, have their main office in The Hague. The idea of the protective wallet was born in the 1990s, but really took off ten years ago when skimming became more prevalent. Secrid, made in Holland, is now available in over 70 countries.

5 charming shops to buy
FLOWERS & PLANTS

246 THE FLOWER KITCHEN

Prins Willem-
straat 32
Scheveningen –
Visserijbuurt ⑤
+31 (0)70 355 61 30
theflowerkitchen.nl

This adorable flower boutique is located in a completely renovated old fire station. The back of the shop, where the owners Steven and Lilith now create beautiful bouquets, once was the place where horse-drawn fire engines stood. Besides flowers, The Flower Kitchen sells plants, cactuses, flower pots and vases.

247 ABOUT FLOWERS

Korte Houtstraat 14
Uilebomen ②
+31 (0)70 362 13 02
aboutflowers.nl

If you want a stunning flower bouquet, go straight to this bright flower shop located in a picturesque alley near Plein. About Flowers sells flowers of the highest quality, and often has unique varieties. Sustainable Florist certified!

248 FILYA INDOOR GARDEN

Fluwelen Burgwal 1-F
Uilebomen ②
+31 (0)6 50 25 45 65
filyaindoorgarden.com

For anyone who wants to create an urban jungle at home, Filya is the place. Glass jar terrariums, hanging kokedama, bonsai trees, Filya has it all. The owner, Daniela, knows everything there is to know about plants: which plants are safe for cats and children, what are the best air-purifying plants? A must-go shop for plant lovers!

249 AU PETIT PONT

Mauritskade
(corner Nieuwe
Schoolstraat)
Voorhout ②
+31 (0)70 346 85 75

This lovely flower kiosk started some 40 years ago on the little bridge at the beginning of Frederikstraat, hence the name. When it grew too big, it moved to this location. The flowers are super fresh and the owner always tries to sell some special varieties as well. On Saturday, it can be crowded here.

250 LITTLE GREEN SHOP

Prins Hendrik-
straat 103
Zeeheldenkwartier ③
+31 (0)6 31 75 58 92
littlegreen-shop.nl

Green up your home and head to this cosy shop full of houseplants and pots. Barro, the owner, will inform you about the right temperature, light and humidity. This way your newly purchased plants will thrive for years to come. Barro is specialised in the Japanese plant art *Kokedama*.

248 FILYA INDOOR GARDEN

CITY HALL OF THE HAGUE

15 BUILDINGS
TO ADMIRE

———

5 remarkable **20TH-CENTURY BUILDINGS** — 138

The 5 most striking examples of
CONTEMPORARY ARCHITECTURE ——— 141

5 places to admire **ART NOUVEAU**
and **ART DECO** ———————————— 144

5 remarkable
20TH-CENTURY
BUILDINGS

251 NIRWANAFLAT

Benoorden-
houtseweg 227
Haagse Hout ⑥

It is hard to believe that after its completion in 1929 the Nirwanaflat was considered the first high-rise of the Netherlands. Its design was based on Het Nieuwe Bouwen (the Modern Movement) and thus rationality, functionality and practicality were among its most important characteristics. The flat was to house well-to-do returnees from the Dutch East Indies, who craved for luxuries such as an in-house restaurant, maids and servants.

252 PAPAVERHOF

Segbroek ⑧

These sober white concrete middle-class houses were built in the design of De Stijl. This Dutch art movement embraced abstraction, geometric forms and primary colours and had famous members like Theo van Doesburg, Piet Mondrian and Gerrit Rietveld. The 1921 complex, with its lush courtyard, was designed by Jan Wils and is now an important Dutch monument.

252 PAPAVERHOF

253 DALTON SCHOOL

Aronskelkweg 1
Loosduinen ⑨

In between the two World Wars, The Hague developed its own architectural style, known as the New Hague School. It has cubism, symmetry and horizontalism in common with its contemporary, the Amsterdam School, but is slightly more luxurious. Examples can be found throughout the city, but the Dalton School by J.J. Brandes stands out.

254 TOREN VAN OUD

Catsheuvel 16
Scheveningen –
Zorgvliet ③

In 1969, the triangular Toren van Oud was considered the first skyscraper of The Hague. As the hotel of the conference centre next door, it never really took off and the Toren van Oud was subsequently turned into an office building. After thorough remodelling, this iconic building will get a new life again, this time as a short-stay apartment building offering 'rooms with a view' only.

255 DE HAAGSE BIJENKORF

Grote Marktstraat 55
Old Centre ①
debijenkorf.nl/
den-haag

In 1924, the luxury department store De Bijenkorf decided to open a branch in The Hague. Thus, it does not come as a surprise that it selected a design by the Amsterdam School architect P.L. Kramer. Although the interior has been completely renovated twice, its padouk wooden staircase with impressive stained glass windows can still be seen in all its glory.

The 5 most striking examples of
CONTEMPORARY
ARCHITECTURE

256 CITY HALL OF THE HAGUE

Spui 70
Uilebomen ②
denhaag.com

When the bright and white City Hall in the centre was completed in 1995, citizens immediately nicknamed it the 'Ice Palace'. The building is designed by the American architect Richard Meier, who is noted for his minimalist white constructions. The tall central space inside, the Atrium, is spectacular and worth a visit. Exhibitions, concerts and events are often organised here (free entrance).

257 STADSKANTOOR & PUBLIC LIBRARY ESCAMP

Leyweg 811-813
Escamp ⑨
+31 (0)70 353 80 30
bibliotheekdenhaag.nl

The 'Second City Hall' of The Hague, which opened in 2011, looks like a giant waffle perched in the ground. With its 75 metres and triangular design by Dutch architect Rudy Uytenhaak, it is the most iconic building in the south-western part of The Hague. It is home to one of the municipality's district offices and to a public library.

258 AMARE

Spuiplein 150
Uilebomen
+31 (0)70 880 03 33
amare.nl

Jo Coenen and Patrick Fransen designed this impressive cultural temple with a dance theatre, concert hall and conservatory. It has four equal façades consisting of rows of 'tuning forks' that blend into a crown-like roof. Solar panels, rainwater collection for flushing toilets, nesting boxes and bat lodges make Amare one of the most sustainable buildings in the city.

259 TURFMARKT AREA SKYLINE

Uilebomen ②

Recently, most of the ministries have relocated to the Turfmarkt area in either new or newly renovated buildings. The ministry of Education ('The Iron') together with the ministries of Justice and of Home Affairs (the two towers called 'JuBi') stand tallest. The so-dubbed 'Hague Tits' (ministries of Employment and of Health) have been voted among the strangest skyscrapers in the world.

260 START AND END STATION E-LINE

Anna van
Buerenplein
Stationsbuurt ②

If you travel from Rotterdam to The Hague by metro, you arrive in what appears to be a spaceship station. Floating high above the ground, made of bended steel and glass, the futuristic E-line metro station catapults you to the next century. The slick design by Zwarts & Jansma Architects is bound to impress for decades to come.

260 **START AND END STATION E-LINE**

264 **LAAN VAN MEERDERVOORT**

5 places to admire
ART NOUVEAU
and ART DECO

---

261 HEILIGE ANTONIUS ABTKERK

Scheveningse-
weg 235
Scheveningen –
Visserijbuurt ⑤
vriendenvandeabt.nl

Unimpressive on the outside, but very expressive on the inside. A group of artists related to symbolism and art deco, is responsible for the rich interior of the Heilige Antonius Abtkerk. Centrepiece is the largest mosaic to be found in the Netherlands by Antoon Molkenboer, depicting Scheveningen residents praying during a cholera outbreak in 1848.

262 NOORDEINDE

Hofkwartier ②

After Brussels, The Hague boasts most art nouveau buildings. Especially high-end retailers, who set up new businesses around 1900 in the fast-growing city, commissioned art nouveau façades and entrances. That is why you find many examples in downtown shopping streets, such as Kettingstraat, Hoogstraat, Korte Poten and, above all, Noordeinde (e.g. at numbers 41-43, 44-46, 164).

263 HUIS VAN LORRIE

Smidswater 26
Voorhout ②

One of the earliest and best-kept examples of Dutch art nouveau, is the so-called House of Lorrie. Not only the façade, but also the interior and the furniture have been designed in this turn-of-the-century style. Architect and contractor Lorrie commissioned the office annex private residence in 1896. Still private today, only the richly decorated exterior is on display. The brass mailbox is probably the most photographed one in town.

264 LAAN VAN MEERDERVOORT

Laan van Meerdervoort 213-237
Scheveningen – Duinoord ③

The impressive row of 13 houses designed by architect Jan Olthuis was constructed in 1900-1901. The limestone façades have been decorated with meandering sculptures with floral motives. Expect curving balconies, half-round windows, merlons, gables, and plenty of ornaments. Vintage art nouveau!

265 HUIS DE ZEEMEEUW

Wagenaarweg 30
Scheveningen – Westbroekpark ⑤

This is truly the most beautiful art nouveau villa in the Netherlands. Exterior and interior have been designed by Belgian architect Henry van de Velde, who created a Total Work of Art. The asymmetric exterior has been moulded around the central hallway and staircase, which have been decorated with a large sgraffito (wall decoration) by Johan Thorn Prikker. Unfortunately, it can only be admired on the outside.

SMIDSWATER / NIEUWE UITLEG

75 PLACES TO DISCOVER THE HAGUE

5 ROYAL PLACES —————————————— 150

The 5 most IMPRESSIVE VIEWS ————————— 152

5 historic HOMES
OF FAMOUS DUTCHMEN ————————— 154

5 places to explore THE INTERNATIONAL
CITY OF PEACE & JUSTICE————————— 156

5 CITY PARKS worth a stroll ———————— 158

The 5 most beautiful 'SECRET' GARDENS ——— 161

The 5 most peaceful HIDDEN PARKS———————— 163

5 interesting places TO COMMEMORATE
WORLD WAR II ——————————————— 165

5 interesting RESIDENTIAL COURTYARDS — 168

5 peaceful HIDDEN STREETS ———————— 171

5 special CHURCHES and CHAPELS ———— 173

5 historical CEMETERIES ———————— 175

5 remarkable THE HAGUE STATUES ———— 178

The 5 most beautiful CANALS ——————— 180

5 remarkable LIBRARIES and ARCHIVES —— 182

5

ROYAL PLACES

266 KNEUTERDIJK PALACE

Kneuterdijk 20
Voorhout ②
+31 (0)70 426 44 26
raadvanstate.nl
denhaag.com

Kneuterdijk Palace breathes Dutch history: it was home to William II and Anna Paulowna, in 1848 the Dutch Constitution was signed here, and after WWII Dutch war criminals were tried on its premises. The early 18th-century palace is now occupied by the Council of State. Free concerts are held in its Gothic Hall.

266 KNEUTERDIJK PALACE

267 ROYAL STABLES

Hogewal 17
Hofkwartier ②
koninklijkhuis.nl

To this day, Dutch royalty comes with horses and carriages. And these 19th-century stables are where they reside. Only during three weeks in summer, the Golden Coach, the Glass Coach and other carriages that are still being used on formal occasions, are on display when the Royal Stables open their doors to the public.

268 HUIS TEN BOSCH PALACE

's-Gravenhaagse Bos 10
Haagse Hout ⑥

This palace, tucked away in the Haagse Bos, is the residence of King Willem-Alexander and Queen Máxima and their daughters. It was originally built in 1645 as a summer palace for Stadholder Frederik Hendrik. Since then, it has often been occupied by members of the royal family.

269 NOORDEINDE PALACE

Noordeinde 68
Hofkwartier ②
koninklijkhuis.nl

Ever since the widow of Prince William of Orange moved in in 1566, on and off Oranges have lived at Noordeinde Palace, and extensive alterations have been made. Since 1984, the palace has functioned as the working palace of the Dutch monarchs. Therefore, the palace can only be visited during three weeks in summer.

270 KLOOSTERKERK

Lange Voorhout 4
Voorhout ②
+31 (0)70 346 15 76
kloosterkerk.nl

The Kloosterkerk dates back to the late Middle Ages. In the 16th century, the catholic church turned protestant and prince Maurits of Orange chose it as his congregation. The special relationship between the Kloosterkerk and the royal family still exists today.

The 5 most
IMPRESSIVE VIEWS

271 LOOKOUT AT VOGELWIJK

AT: WESTDUINPARK
Cort van der
Lindenpad
Segbroek ⑤
westduinpark.nl

The highest dune in the middle of a broad stretch of dunes called Westduinpark on the south side of the city offers impressive views of this nature reserve and the coastline. The eleven kilometres of sandy beaches come in full view.

272 DE PIER

Strandweg
Scheveningen –
Beach ⑤
+31 (0)6 10 38 68 59
pier.nl

At the iconic 1961 Pier you can climb the watchtower daily. If enjoying the view is not exciting enough for you, either bungee jump or zip from the top. Alternatively, make the rounds at 'Europe's first Ferris wheel over the sea', built in 2016.

273 VUURTOREN

Zeekant 12
Scheveningen –
Beach ⑤
+31 (0)70 350 08 30
muzeescheveningen.nl

In 1875, the Scheveningen Lighthouse replaced the fires that the wives of fishermen lit on the beach to guide their husbands home. The cast iron tower, almost 55 metres high, had a reach of over 50 kilometres. Twice a week, the Muzee museum organises guided tours, which not only provide a beautiful sea view, but also a glimpse into forgone times.

274 THE HAGUE TOWER OF THE GROTE KERK

Rond de
Grote Kerk 12
Old Centre ①
+31 (0)70 747 01 02
gadenhaag.nl
dehaagsetoren.nl

What do Vincent van Gogh and Napoleon have in common? They both climbed the 288 steps of the Hague Tower to enjoy the spectacular views from its balcony. Follow in their footsteps and admire the old city, the new skyline, the coast, and on clear days even the cities of Leiden and Rotterdam from this six-centuries-old church tower.

275 THE HARBOUR CLUB

Binckhorstlaan 36
Laak ⑦
+31 (0)70 891 32 24
theharbourclub.com

A large restaurant with a fabulous terrace overlooking metropolitan The Hague is awaiting you when you reach the fifth floor of this industrial building. The interior is somewhat over the top and the food Japanese-inspired. The restaurant regularly turns into a club, so dine and dance with a view of the increasingly impressing skyline of the city.

274 THE HAGUE TOWER OF THE GROTE KERK

5 historic
HOMES OF FAMOUS DUTCHMEN

276 LOUIS COUPERUS

Surinamestraat 20
Archipel ④

Couperus documented life in upper-class The Hague around the turn of the 19th century, but he is also famous for his psychological and historic novels (available in English). He wrote *Eline Vere* (the Dutch *Madame Bovary*) in his father's house at Surinamestraat 20. The house is private property, so to learn more about the writer and his work, visit the Louis Couperus Museum at Javastraat 17.

277 DOMUS SPINOZANA

Paviljoens-
gracht 72-74
Chinatown ①
+31 (0)6 10 01 12 15
spinozahuis.nl

The leading philosopher of the Dutch Golden Age, Baruch Spinoza, wrote his most important work *Ethics* in the attic of Paviljoensgracht 72-74, where he lived from 1670 to 1677 and died. The house does not offer tours, but the library, containing many editions of his work and numerous books on the philosopher, is open to the public every Monday between 2 and 4 pm.

278 JAN VAN GOYEN HOUSE

Dunne Bierkade 16
Chinatown ①
+31 (0)70 322 04 87
buitenmuseum.com

Three famous 17th-century painters settled at the Dunne Bierkade. Landscape painter Jan van Goyen owned a house at number 16, where he took in Jan Steen, painter of interiors and rowdy scenes and his son-in-law. Paulus Potter, famous for landscapes and cattle, lived and worked in the house next door. For groups, visits to the Jan van Goyen House can be arranged through the Buitenmuseum.

279 CATSHUIS

Adriaan Goekoop-
laan 10
Scheveningen –
Zorgvliet ③

Poet and politician Jacob Cats took up residence in the middle of park Sorghvliet in 1652. Later, the Catshuis was owned by Dutch nobility and even royalty. Now the official residence of the Dutch Prime Minister, the Catshuis is mainly used to host meetings for ministers and to receive eminent guests. If you're neither, it can only be viewed from a distance.

280 HUYGENS' HOFWIJCK

Westeinde 2-A
Voorburg ⑦
+31 (0)70 387 23 11
hofwijck.nl

Two famous men of the 17th century lived here. Constantijn Huygens (poet, writer, composer, politician, diplomat) had Hofwijck built as a summer escape. Later his son Christiaan (astronomer, physicist, mathematician, inventor) took up residence. Hofwijck is now a charming museum where you can admire paintings, works of both men, inventions of Christiaan, and the lovely garden.

5 places to explore
THE INTERNATIONAL CITY OF PEACE & JUSTICE

---

281 PEACE PALACE

Carnegieplein 2
Scheveningen –
Zorgvliet ④
+31 (0)70 302 42 42
vredespaleis.nl

Made possible by donations from steel baron Andrew Carnegie, the Peace Palace was built after the 1899 Hague Peace Conference to provide a home for the Permanent Court of Arbitration and the Library of International Law. Today it also hosts the UN's International Court of Justice. A guided tour through the splendid rooms of the palace is a must-do. And do not miss the historical garden tour in summer.

282 INTERNATIONAL CRIMINAL COURT

Oude Waals-
dorperweg 10
Scheveningen –
Oostduinen ⑤
+31 (0)70 515 85 15
icc-cpi.int

Acknowledging that after war there cannot be lasting peace without bringing war criminals to justice, the International Criminal Court was established in 2002. The Court puts much emphasis on giving victims a voice and involving effected communities. Court hearings are often open to the public and visitors are welcome to explore the ICC exhibit, gardens and cafe.

283 EUROPOL

Eisenhowerlaan 73
Scheveningen –
Zorgvliet ③
+31 (0)70 302 50 00
europol.europa.eu

The Hague hosts the EU institution Europol, responsible for police cooperation. Law enforcement officers from the EU member states collaborate here in the fight against terrorism, cybercrime, and other large-scale and cross-border criminal activity. Eurojust, where prosecutors and judges work together on these issues, is just across the street. Study tours for small groups are available upon request.

284 THE INTERNATIONAL RESIDUAL MECHANISM FOR CRIMINAL TRIBUNALS

Churchillplein 1
Scheveningen –
Zorgvliet ③
+31 (0)70 512 58 75
irmct.org

The International Residual Mechanism for Criminal Tribunals houses in the former premises of the now closed Yugoslavia Tribunal. It still hears cases related to the ad hoc Yugoslavia and Rwanda Tribunals that were created to prosecute and try those responsible for the atrocities committed in the early nineties. Court hearings can be attended by the public. The scheduled dates of hearings can be found on the website.

285 OPCW

Johan de Wittlaan 32
Scheveningen –
Zorgvliet ③
+31 (0)70 416 33 00
opcw.org

In 2013, the Organisation for the Prohibition of Chemical Weapons earned the Nobel Peace Prize for its efforts to free the world of chemical weapons. Its headquarters occupy the cylinder-shaped building in the International Zone. OPCW staff members regularly provide public presentations. The Nobel Peace Prize is also on display.

5

CITY PARKS

worth a stroll

---

286 ZUIDERPARK
Escamp ⑨

Bring your own barbecue, as many locals do, or go for a stroll or a skate in what many consider 'the people's park' of The Hague. Zuiderpark has a large indoor swimming pool, a model steam train and an outdoor theatre, too. Nonetheless, there is still enough nature to enjoy: its arboretum even contains over 700 species from around the world.

287 WESTBROEKPARK
Scheveningen –
Westbroekpark ⑤

Westbroekpark counts large green fields where you can picnic, barbecue and play soccer. Ten thousands of roses peak in late summer and early autumn, making a visit to the Rose Garden mandatory that time of the year. Rent a boat at tearoom the Waterkant. Or visit one of many outdoor events, such as theatre festival De Parade or food truck festival TREK.

288 SCHEVENINGSE BOSJES

Scheveningen – Scheveningse Bosjes ③⑤

This dune landscape is still relatively young. In the Middle Ages, it consisted of sand only, and to stop its expansion into the young city, trees and vegetation were planted. The dune forest almost disappeared during WWII, when residents needed the wood to survive. Thanks to replanting, the park survived. Great for strolling, running, horse riding and taking the kids out.

289 PARK CLINGENDAEL

Haagse Hout ⑥

Originally, the park belonged to the Clingendael estate, home to Dutch nobility. During WWII, the head of the Nazi-occupied Netherlands, Arthur Seyss-Inquart, took up residence and had a bunker built camouflaged as a farm. The gardens are designed in the style of 19th-century English landscaping.

287 / WESTBROEKPARK

290 **PALEISTUIN**

Prinsessewal
Hofkwartier ②

You can hardly get closer to Dutch royalty than in this now public park between Noordeinde Palace and the Royal Stables. It was created around 1600 and has been remodelled many times since to suit changing fashion and taste. Today, find modern artworks and a playground, royal cool on hot summer days, and greens and benches to enjoy a picnic.

The 5 most beautiful
'SECRET' GARDENS

---

291 DE KORNOELJE

Kornoeljestraat 117
Segbroek ⑧
+31 (0)70 353 29 96

A bunch of freshly picked flowers. Who doesn't like that? In summer, it's permitted to pick flowers from the beautiful garden of Kornoelje, a community garden in the Vruchtenbuurt. Twenty stems only cost one euro. Find one of the volunteers to explain how it works. And don't forget to bring your own pair of scissors.

292 EMMA'S HOF

Galileïstraat 36
Segbroek ⑧
emmashof.nl

A mosaic bench à la Gaudi, a tiny stream, sloping garden paths, a white wooden teahouse. This small hidden garden, created by residents in the heart of the Regentessewijk, is the green pearl of the neighbourhood and certainly one of the prettiest in town. It's a perfect place to read a book or have a glass of wine with friends.

293 NUTSTUIN

Riviervismarkt 5
Old Centre ①
+31 (0)70 345 90 90
nutshuis.nl

This organic garden is situated in downtown The Hague and therefore an excellent place to escape the hustle and bustle of the city. It boasts a pond, fruit trees, a greenhouse, and the relaxed Juni Café with a lovely terrace. In August, you can watch open-air movies on a large outdoor screen here.

294 JAPANESE GARDEN

AT: PARK CLINGENDAEL
Wassenaarseweg
Haagse Hout ⑥
denhaag.nl

The oldest Japanese garden in the Netherlands is only open to the public in spring and autumn. This fragile garden, situated in Park Clingendael and a national monument, was created more than a century ago by Marguérite M. Baroness van Brienen (1871-1939), who lived on the estate. She travelled to Japan several times and brought back plants, lanterns, sculptures and a little bridge.

295 GARDEN BEHIND THE KUNSTMUSEUM DEN HAAG

Stadhouderslaan 41
Scheveningen –
Zorgvliet ③
+31 (0)70 338 11 11
kunstmuseum.nl

Stroll around the magnificent Kunstmuseum building by architect Berlage (formerly known as the Gemeentemuseum Den Haag) and you'll discover a large back garden with several sculptures. The garden is symmetrical with a pergola that leads to a small building originally designed as the museum's lunchroom. This lunchroom, a novelty in the 1930s, is now Brasserie Berlage.

The 5 most peaceful
HIDDEN PARKS

---

296 SINT HUBERTUSPARK

Plesmanweg
Scheveningen –
Duttendel ⑤

Hidden behind busy thoroughfares, an overpass and military barracks lies Sint Hubertuspark. Once a dune area and hunting grounds on the outskirts of The Hague, it was transformed into a park in the early 1930s. One of its dunes was raised in height and fitted with stairs by the then-unemployed, 'with their blood, sweat and tears'. This nicknamed Bloedberg (blood mountain) offers unexpected views over the city.

297 PARK SORGHVLIET

Scheveningseweg 24-A
Scheveningen –
Zorgvliet ③
+31 (0)6 18 30 45 53
*rijksvastgoedbedrijf.nl/
parksorghvliet*

Park Sorghvliet is not for everyone! Buy yourself an annual pass at the tourist office and you'll be one of the happy few that can enjoy the walled-in park created in 1643 by poet and politician Jacob Cats. Here you can find quiet and solitude and enjoy the French- and English-style landscape architecture, not to mention the foxes, owls, numerous kinds of nesting birds, and bees.

298 BURGEMEESTER DE MONCHYPLEIN
Archipel ④

Now surrounded by a modern apartment complex designed by postmodern architect Ricardo Bofill, this square was formerly the site of fairs, demonstrations and soldiers marching, and of the post-war city hall. The public garden consists of a large pond, a waterfall, greens and trees. Entering from one of the surrounding 19th-century streets, you suddenly find yourself in a completely different environment.

299 SUNNY COURT
Laan van Meerdervoort 189-B
Scheveningen – Duinoord ③

A small gate, in a half-circular block of houses, gives way to a small park popular with local young families. Children run around freely and climb the wooden playground equipment, while their parents catch up on the latest neighbourhood gossip. Every now and then, the park is the site of small-scale music festivals or neighbourhood events.

300 ARENDSDORP & PARK OOSTDUIN
Wassenaarseweg
Haagse Hout ⑥

Arendsdorp is named after nobleman Arend van Dorp, who acquired the land and its farm in 1586. Later, a gardener's house, a tea pavilion and a fish pond were added to the estate, and in 1845 adjacent Park Oostduin as well. In this estate-turned-public-park, you can go for a stroll, take the kids to the playground, read a book, or organise a picnic.

5 interesting places
TO COMMEMORATE WORLD WAR II

301 **RABBIJN MAARSENPLEIN**
Chinatown ①

The square, named after the Chief Rabbi of The Hague who died in a concentration camp during WWII, is situated in the former Jewish Quarter. This poor neighbourhood was deserted in 1943 when all remaining Jews were transported out of The Hague, many of them to concentration camps. The Jewish Children Monument commemorates the more than 2000 Jewish children from The Hague who never returned.

302 **WAALSDORPER-VLAKTE**
AT: MEIJENDEL PARK
Wassenaar –
Suburbs North ⑥

Over 250 members of the Dutch resistance were executed in this open area in the middle of Meijendel, the dune park bordering Scheveningen in the north. Four bronze crosses and a giant bell honour these men and women. Annually, on May 4 during Remembrance Day, all victims of war are commemorated here in a solemn and silent march. The site can be visited year-round.

303 NATIONAAL MONUMENT ORANJEHOTEL

Van Alkemade-
laan 1258
Scheveningen –
Belgisch Park ⑤
+31 (0)70 222 80 70
oranjehotel.org

The German occupier used Scheveningen prison to incarcerate and interrogate over 25.000 suspected members of the Dutch resistance. Hence the nickname Oranjehotel (Hotel Orange). Not much of a hotel, the cells were small and always overcrowded with a wide array of prisoners: politicians, resistance fighters, secret agents and intellectuals among them. 'Death cell 601' is still intact and at the heart of the remembrance centre, now open to the public.

304 INDISCH MONUMENT

AT: SCHEVENINGSE
BOSJES
Scheveningen –
Scheveningse
Bosjes ⑤
+31 (0)70 200 25 05
15augustus1945.nl

For the Dutch East Indies, WWII did not end until 15 August 1945, when Japan capitulated to the Allied Forces. During the Japanese occupation, 17.000 civilians and 8500 prisoners of war died in camps or while building railroads throughout South East Asia. It took the Netherlands quite some time to commemorate these victims, and the Indisch Monument wasn't unveiled until 1988.

305 VILLA WINDEKIND

Nieuwe Parklaan 76
Scheveningen –
Westbroekpark ⑤

This private residence was commissioned in the late twenties by Queen Wilhelmina's confidant Van't Sant. In 1942, the Van't Sant family had to turn the villa over to the German Security Police, who used it as its headquarters for the inquisition and deportation of Jewish residents. To this end, the rooms on the lower floors were turned into horrific torture chambers.

302 WAALSDORPERVLAKTE

5 interesting
RESIDENTIAL
COURTYARDS

---

306 HEILIGE GEEST HOFJE

Paviljoensgracht 125
Old Centre ①
hetheiligegeesthofje.nl

Even after more than four centuries, this residential courtyard (*hofje*) still offers low-income singles of over 45 years old a place to live. You can visit the oldest *hofje* of The Hague during the annual Heritage Day or by renting a room in the guesthouse. Marvel at its early 17th-century architecture and admire the oldest pear tree in the Netherlands, planted in 1647.

307 RUSTHOF

Parkstraat 41-61
Voorhout ②
+31 (0)70 360 51 63
hofjerusthof.nl

An unassuming green door on a busy thoroughfare gives access to an intimate world of quietude. The catholic church next door towers high over the small private quarters. Since its opening in 1841, the Rusthof has housed single protestant women with a modest income. Open daily from 10 am to 5 pm, but do respect the privacy of the inhabitants.

308 'T HOOFTSHOFJE

Assendelftstraat 85
Old Centre ⓘ
hooftshofje.nl

The fortunate Angenis Hooft had determined that her inheritance was to be spent on the construction of charity housing for 16 single, reformed women. For that purpose, 't Hooftshofje was built in 1756. Her fortune was large enough to allow the women occupying the premises between 1757 and 1952 to live there for free. 't Hooftshofje can be visited through Gilde Den Haag city tours.

309 HOF VAN WOUW

Lange Beesten-
markt 49-85
Old Centre ⓘ
hofvanwouw.nl

This residential courtyard has maintained its 17th-century vibe. The rules for being granted residence in the Hof van Wouw haven't changed either since they were drafted by Cornelia van Wouw in 1647: only single women over 50 are allowed to live here. The Hof van Wouw organises several public events throughout the year.

310 HOFJE VAN NIEUWKOOP

Warmoezier-
straat 44-206
Old Centre ⓘ
hofjevannieuwkoop.nl

From the outside, it has the appearance of a fortress, but its inhabitants refer to it as 'a village in the city'. It counts 62 small houses, all with red blinds, around a large green courtyard. Hofje van Nieuwkoop is different in that it is much larger and slightly more liberal than other residential courtyards. Open to the public on Heritage Days.

306 HEILIGE GEEST HOFJE

311 WERFSTRAAT

5 *peaceful*
HIDDEN STREETS

---

311 WERFSTRAAT, ZEILSTRAAT, ANKERSTRAAT

Scheveningen – Beach ⑤

Visit these picturesque small streets in Scheveningen if you want to get an impression of what this fishing village looked like at the end of the 19th century. The tiny houses you find here, were built for the fishermen's families in a time that Scheveningen was growing rapidly due to the scale increase of the fishing industry.

312 SPINOZASTRAATJE

Chinatown ①

In between Dunne Bierkade 26 and 29, a small gate gives entrance to a charming private alleyway, locally known as the Spinozastraatje. Rumour has it that around 1670 this back alley was used by the protestant political leader of the Dutch Republic Johan de Witt when secretly seeking advice from Jewish philosopher Spinoza, who lived around the corner.

313 VAN OSTADESTRAAT, HANNEMANSTRAAT, JACOB CATSSTRAAT

Schilderswijk ⑨

Dubbed the best kept secret of The Hague, these three small and peaceful streets in the middle of the Schilderswijk, look nothing like the neighbourhood around them. The houses, called the Van Ostade-woningen, had been commissioned around 1890 by well-off Jews to help less fortunate Jewish workers. Since the synagogue was quite far away, anyone with a modest income was welcomed, and that still is the case today.

314 MALLEMOLEN, SCHUDDEGEEST

Archipel ④

These cute little streets have very different origins. While the barracks at the Mallemolen were built to house Napoleon's soldiers, the homes at the Schuddegeest are one of the earliest examples of social housing for workers. Between 1945 and 1972, many well-known Dutch artists settled at the Mallemolen and the small streets were nicknamed 'Little Montmartre'.

315 VAN STOLKWEG, PARKWEG, HOGEWEG

Scheveningen –
Scheveningse
Bosjes ⑤

Stroll through the quiet streets behind the Scheveningseweg and marvel at the grandiose villas dating back to around 1900 in this secluded forested inner dune area. Attorney Van Stolk had this villa park (Van Stolkpark) designed by Jan David and Louis Paul Zocher, after the introduction of the horse tram had made the area more accessible. Many of the villas are on the list of national monuments.

5 special
CHURCHES and CHAPELS

316 RUSSIAN CHURCH

Obrechtstraat 9
Scheveningen –
Duinoord ③
+31 (0)6 41 52 54 42
ruskerkdenhaag.
wordpress.com

Before Anna Pavlovna, widow of Dutch King William II, died in 1865, she determined that her dowry of religious objects would remain in the Netherlands, under the condition that they would be used during Russian-Orthodox ceremonies. Fifty years later, in this small chapel her religious belongings found shelter. They are on display during weekend services.

317 OLD-CATHOLIC CLANDESTINE CHURCH

Juffrouw Idastraat 7
Hofkwartier ②
denhaag.okkn.nl

In the 16th century, Catholicism in The Hague was only practised in hidden attics like the one at Juffrouw Idastraat. Over a century later, Catholics were again allowed to build churches, as long as they were not visible from the street. Behind this clandestine church, the St James and Augustine Church was built. Guided tours are available on Saturdays at 2.30 pm. Entrance at Molenstraat 44.

318 WILLIBRORDUS HOUSE

Oude Molstraat 35
Hofkwartier ②
+31 (0)70 365 43 85
monasticstore.nl

When in 1581 Catholics were forced out of the Grote Kerk, they found refuge in a home at the Oude Molstraat. It was later transformed into a monastery, occupied today by the Brothers of Saint John. In 1928, a beautiful chapel with stained-glass windows and wall paintings was added. It can be visited through the monastic store that sells the Haagsche Broeder beer, brewed on site.

319 MARANATHAKERK

2e Sweelinck-
straat 156
Scheveningen –
Duinoord ③
+31 (0)70 345 91 19
*maranatha
kerkdenhaag.nl*

After WWII, Bauhaus architect Otto Bartning designed temporary churches that were sent as a do-it-yourself kit to devastated cities around Germany. Thanks to a Swiss protestant relief organisation, one ended up in The Hague and was built up at a site were the German occupier had torn down houses to construct the Atlantikwall. The 'temporary' Maranatha church is now an important monument.

320 ABDIJKERK / ABBEY CHURCH

Willem III straat 40
Loosduinen ⑨
+31 (0)70 397 41 82
abdijkerk.nl

The surrounding buildings don't give away that, yes, this is The Hague's oldest building still standing. It has been around since 1250, was almost completely destroyed except for its tower at the end of the 16th century, and was rebuilt using stones from the fallen walls. In summer the church is open to the public on Sunday afternoons, organ recital included.

5 historical
CEMETERIES

---

321 JEWISH CEMETERY

Scheveningseweg
Scheveningen –
Scheveningse
Bosjes ④
joodsebegraafplaats.nl

Behind an old wall opposite the Peace Palace around 10.000 Ashkenazi and Sephardic Jews are buried. They found their eternal rest at this extensive cemetery between 1694 and 1908, only to be disturbed during WWII when the Germans dug trenches and the British accidentally dropped a bomb on the cemetery. Requests for guided tours can be made through the website.

322 OUD EIK EN DUINEN

Laan van Eik en
Duinen
Segbroek ⑧
+31 (0)70 447 00 00
*monuta.nl/vestiging/
begraafplaats-
oudeikenduinen*

The gravestones at Oud Eik en Duinen whisper the history of the city of The Hague. Many of its prominent administrators, politicians, nobles, painters, writers and poets can be found here. Created in 1247 as the tiny cemetery of a hamlet far out in the fields, it has grown extensively over the years. Now it's a green oasis sandwiched between residential areas.

323 TER NAVOLGING

Prins Willem-
straat 43
Scheveningen –
Old Town ⑤
ternavolging.nl

This is one of the most hidden cemeteries of The Hague! Breaking with the Dutch tradition to bury the Christian dead in or near the downtown churches, Ter Navolging was created in the late 18th century in the dunes outside the city centre out of hygienic concerns. This small cemetery, resembling a church without a roof, is a quiet oasis in the now bustling Scheveningen.

324 ST. PETRUS BANDEN

Kerkhoflaan 10
Archipel ④
+31 (0)70 350 37 18
*begraafplaats
stpetrusbanden.nl*

With its neoclassical chapel, its neo-romantic arcade, its byzantine influences and its cross-shaped layout, St. Petrus Banden cemetery is unmistakably Roman Catholic. Visit one of the most beautiful cemeteries on a summer day and you might think you were in Italy. Since 1830, many Catholic public figures from The Hague have been buried here.

325 ALGEMENE BEGRAAFPLAATS KERKHOFLAAN

Kerkhoflaan 12
Archipel ④
+31 (0)70 350 40 36

In the early 1900s, fear of suspended animation grew, thus spurring the design of houses where the deceased were kept with an ingenious alarm system within reach. One can still be found at the municipal cemetery Kerkhoflaan. On its premises, you will also find monuments remembering the fallen men of the 1940 Battle of The Hague and the victims of the 1945 Bezuidenhout bombing.

5 remarkable
THE HAGUE STATUES

326 VISSERSMONUMENT – DE SCHEVENINGSE VROUW
Kalhuisplaats
Scheveningen – Beach ⑤

For centuries, the main source of income in Scheveningen village was fishery. The men sailed the seas, while their wives stayed behind. After heavy storms, the women would be scanning the horizons hoping that their loved-ones would return safely. Gerard Bakker designed this statue in 1982 in honour of the fishermen's wives.

327 WILHELMINA
Paleisstraat 1-A
Hofkwartier ②

In this 1987 statue opposite Noordeinde Palace, sculptor Charlotte van Pallandt pictures Queen Wilhelmina as many came to see her during WWII, as the unbending Mother of the Resistance. Wilhelmina reigned the kingdom for about 50 years and in the last years of her life, wrote her autobiography *Eenzaam maar niet alleen* (*Lonely but not Alone*). These words are written on the wall behind the statue.

328 ELINE VERE
Groot Hertoginnelaan
Scheveningen – Zorgvliet ③

Eline Vere, a famous personage in Louis Couperus's naturalist novel by the same name, was a young upper-class woman destined to die young. Theo van der Nahmer immortalised her in 1948.

329 HAAGS JANTJE

Lange Vijverberg
Voorhout ②

A famous Dutch nursery rhyme recounts the story of little Jan, son of count Floris V, who points out where in The Hague his father lives (spoiler: at the Binnenhof). As the rhyme goes, he points with his hand, has a plume on his hat and carries a basket, just as Ivo Coljé depicts him in the statue overlooking the Hofvijver.

330 LOUIS COUPERUS

Lange Voorhout
Archipel ④

No better place to picture fin-de-siècle, dandy writer Louis Couperus than at the Lange Voorhout where he liked to stroll, to see and be seen. The famous Dutch writer was a cosmopolitan, who always came back to the city he loved (to hate). Kees Verkade recreated his image in bronze in 1998.

326 VISSERSMONUMENT – DE SCHEVENINGSE VROUW

The 5 most beautiful
CANALS

---

331 AFVOERKANAAL

Around Suezkade
Scheveningen –
Duinoord ③

Because of a lack of water flow, the canals of The Hague were a major source of diseases. Hence, in 1888 the Afvoerkanaal was dug for drainage. Subsequently, along the canal, that ran through an extensive dune area, first a school and then blocks of houses were built. These blocks all had different architects, giving way to a playful, and now protected, cityscape.

331 AFVOERKANAAL

332 SMIDSWATER / NIEUWE UITLEG
Voorhout ②

This canal was dug in the 17th century as part of the defensive perimeter around the city. Predominantly farriers and blacksmiths settled here in the houses and stables lining the Smidswater side of the canal. When in the 18th century the city spread beyond the canal, mansions were built on the Nieuwe Uitleg side, which transformed it into the upper-class neighbourhood it still is today.

333 (DUNNE) BIERKADE
Chinatown ①

This is where in the 17th century beer and thin beer (for consumption during breakfast) entered the city of The Hague. Today, the canal is the bustling scene of beer bars, (boat) terraces and restaurants.

334 HARINGKADE
Scheveningen –
Westbroekpark ⑤

The lush Haringkade was part of a canal that connected the city centre to the North Sea. It was constructed between 1825 and 1862 in an attempt to make The Hague a sea port city. That never materialised, but the canal was used to deliver fresh *haring* (herring).

335 TOUSSAINTKADE
Zeeheldenkwartier ④

In the 17th century this canal was part of the defence work against approaching enemies. Now one side of the canal with its 18th-century homes houses several prominent galleries.

5 remarkable
LIBRARIES and
ARCHIVES

---

336 HANDELINGENKAMER

Lange Poten 4
Voorhout ②
+31 (0)70 318 22 11
tweedekamer.nl

The former building of the Ministry of Justice, now part of the premises of parliament, hides an impressive library containing all proceedings of the House of Representatives of the past two centuries. Nine metres and four stories high, a glass window roof, cast iron spiral staircases and many Chinese influences make the wait for one of the rare occasions that it opens to the public worthwhile.

337 PEACE PALACE LIBRARY

Carnegieplein 2
Scheveningen –
Zorgvliet ④
+31 (0)70 302 42 42
peacepalacelibrary.nl

Since 1913, the library has collected over a million titles in the field of international law, making it the oldest and largest international law library in the world. It also has an impressive collection of works by the father of international law, Hugo Grotius. The library is open to all 'students' of international law.

338 MUSEUM VOORLINDEN LIBRARY

Buurtweg 90
Wassenaar –
Suburbs North ⑥
+31 (0)70 512 16 60
voorlinden.nl

This art library doesn't just consist of books on artists but also of artists' books from different times and art genres. Over 40.000 publications on the artists in the museum's collection are lined up from top to bottom and lit by lights shining up from the shelves. In between, showcases display the books designed by artists.

339 NATIONAAL ARCHIEF

Prins Willem-
Alexanderhof 20
Stationsbuurt ②
+31 (0)70 331 54 00
nationaalarchief.nl

Drawing from 137 km of documents, 15 million photographs and nearly 300.000 historical maps and drawings, the National Archives of the Netherlands regularly put together exhibitions exploring Dutch national history. Gain access to the Dutch national memory by visiting an exhibition, conducting research, booking a tour, or even organising a birthday party for the young.

340 MEERMANNO MINIATURE LIBRARY

AT: MUSEUM MEERMANNO
Prinsessegracht 30
Voorhout ②
+31 (0)70 346 27 00
meermanno.nl

Bring your magnifying glass! The Bibliotheca Thurkowiana Minor consists of 1515 tiny books no larger than 3 inches, published and brought together by Guus and Luce Thurkow. The library is inspired by doll's houses for adults, which were popular among the Dutch elite in the 17th century. A secret bookcase containing erotica is only accessible under strict supervision.

MUSEUM BEELDEN AAN ZEE

50 PLACES TO ENJOY CULTURE

The 5 most inspiring ART MUSEUMS —————— 186

5 museums AROUND HET BINNENHOF —— 189

The 5 best SPECIALISED MUSEUMS ———— 192

5 COSY THEATRES ————————————— 194

5 contemporary ARTS & MOVIE CENTRES —— 196

The 5 best ANNUAL FESTIVALS and FAIRS — 198

5 great places for LIVE MUSIC ——————— 200

The 5 best ways to discover INTERNATIONAL
DANCE CITY THE HAGUE —————————— 202

The 5 best places to spot STREET ART
and MURALS ———————————————— 204

5 remarkable PIECES
OF MODERN PUBLIC ART ——————————— 206

The 5 most inspiring
ART MUSEUMS

---

341 KM21 & FOTO-MUSEUM DEN HAAG
Stadhouderslaan 43
Scheveningen –
Zorgvliet ③
+31 (0)70 338 11 11
km21.nl
fotomuseumdenhaag.nl

Two museums under one roof. KM21 organises visual arts exhibitions featuring contemporary young talent. The Fotomuseum offers temporary exhibitions of photographers of the past as well as the present, such as Sally Mann, Emmy Andriesse, Anton Corbijn, Man Ray and Erwin Olaf.

342 MUSEUM BEELDEN AAN ZEE / SCULPTURES BY THE SEA
Harteveltstraat 1
Scheveningen –
Beach ⑤
+31 (0)70 358 58 57
beeldenaanzee.nl

In the dune underneath the pavilion that King William I built for his wife, Theo and Lida Scholten created a beautiful museum for their sculpture collection. Expect modern and contemporary sculptures of international fame. With its smart design and outside terraces overlooking the sea, the building alone is worth a visit.

343 MUSEUM VOORLINDEN

Buurtweg 90
Wassenaar –
Suburbs North ⑥
+31 (0)70 512 16 60
voorlinden.nl

This modern, airy museum is built on an old estate just outside The Hague and houses the largest private art collection in the Netherlands, the so called Caldic Collection of Joop van Caldenborgh. Some captivating artworks on permanent display are works by world-renowned modern and contemporary artists like James Turrell, Richard Serra, Song Dong and Ron Mueck. The museum also hosts cutting-edge art exhibitions.

343 MUSEUM VOORLINDEN

344 PANORAMA MESDAG

Zeestraat 65
Willemspark ④
+31 (0)70 310 66 65
panorama-mesdag.nl

Stepping into this cylindrical painting is like stepping into a life-size 1881 Scheveningen: fishermen at sea, ships ashore, and the city of the Hague in the distance. The Hague School painter Mesdag captured the image while standing on a dune, and a visit to this museum is like standing there next to him. Many of these so-called cycloramas have disappeared, but Mesdag managed to save his from destruction.

345 KUNSTMUSEUM DEN HAAG / THE HAGUE ART MUSEUM

Stadhouderslaan 41
Scheveningen –
Zorgvliet ③
+31 (0)70 338 11 11
kunstmuseum.nl

The Kunstmuseum, until recently known as the Gemeentemuseum, is famous for its extensive Mondrian collection and leading exhibitions. However, the impressive contemporary art, fashion and decorative art collection is not the only attraction. The museum building itself is also very inspiring. It's one of the best works of architect Berlage and a real showpiece. The daylit galleries, the impressive entrance hall, the marble floors, the coloured tiles: this intimate art temple is a must-visit.

5 museums

AROUND HET BINNENHOF

---

346 MAURITSHUIS
Plein 29
Voorhout ②
+31 (0)70 302 34 56
mauritshuis.nl

Not exactly a hidden secret, this museum is world-famous for masterpieces from the Dutch Golden Age like Vermeer's *Girl with a Pearl Earring* and *The Anatomy Lesson of Dr. Nicolaes Tulp* by Rembrandt. However, it has some modern surprises in store as well! Enjoy the colourful ceiling mural by Ger Lataster, *Icarus Atlanticus: Allegory of Human Vanity* (1987), and marvel at the stunning renovation of the building with its underground expansion.

347 GALLERY PRINCE WILLIAM V
Buitenhof 33
Hofkwartier ②
+31 (0)70 302 34 56
mauritshuis.nl

A hidden gem and one of the oldest museums in the Netherlands. In 1774, Prince William V of Orange-Nassau had the museum built to show his art collection to the public. Just like in the old days, the walls are filled to the brim with masterpieces by Steen, Rubens, Potter, among others. The collection is part of the Mauritshuis.

348 MUSEUM DE GEVANGENPOORT / PRISON GATE MUSEUM

Buitenhof 33
Hofkwartier ②
+31 (0)70 346 08 61
gevangenpoort.nl

Up until the 15th century, the Prison Gate was the innocent entrance gate to the castle of the Counts of Holland, now known as the Binnenhof. In 1428, the building became a prison and remained one for 400 years. A place where the accused awaited their sentence, which could entail a fine, banishment, or worse, torture or death. Discover the cruelties of the past during a 30-minute guided tour.

349 THE HISTORICAL MUSEUM OF THE HAGUE

Korte Vijverberg 7
Voorhout ②
+31 (0)70 364 69 40
haagshistorisch
museum.nl

Government city, royal city, and international city of peace and justice. Find out more about the long and intriguing history of The Hague at this museum. The collection is quite diverse with paintings by old masters, antique doll's houses, and, bizarrely enough, the severed tongue and finger of murdered politicians Johan and Cornelis de Witt.

350 MUSEUM BREDIUS

Lange Vijverberg 14
Voorhout ②
+31 (0)70 362 07 29
museumbredius.nl

In 1946, art historian and collector Bredius left his collection of Dutch Golden Age paintings by Rembrandt, Jan Steen, Van Ruisdael, Van Ostade and many others to the municipality of The Hague. The collection can now be viewed in the homely ambiance of an 18th-century townhouse overlooking the Hofvijver and the Binnenhof.

350 **MUSEUM BREDIUS**

The 5 best
SPECIALISED MUSEUMS

---

351 **LOUWMAN MUSEUM**
Leidsestraatweg 57
Haagse Hout ⑥
+31 (0)70 304 73 73
louwmanmuseum.nl

The private collection of the Louwman family holds more than 250 of the funniest, fastest and rarest cars around. Among them James Bond's Aston Martin, the iconic DB5 from the movie *Goldfinger*, and famous winners of the infamous 24 Hours of Le Mans. Even if you are not that much into cars, this museum is a must.

352 **THE HAGUE PUBLIC TRANSPORT MUSEUM**
Parallelweg 224
Schilderswijk ⑨
hovm.nl

Between 1908 and 1983, this was the depot of tram company HTM. Now it's the public transport museum of The Hague housing numerous trams from the past century. Included in the museum's entrance fee is a tour through The Hague in a creaking and squeaking tram of yesteryear. Only open on Sundays, from April through October.

353 ATLANTIKWALL MUSEUM SCHEVENINGEN

Badhuisweg, around nrs. 119-133 Scheveningen – Duttendel ⑤
atlantikwallmuseum.nl

Experience life in a German bunker, Widerstandsnest 318, ordered from Hitler's 'house architect' Albert Speer's bunker catalogue. Widerstandsnest 318 was part of the Atlantikwall that ran all the way from Norway to Spain, straight through the city of The Hague. Most bunkers have been demolished, but this one still stands and is open to the public on Sundays.

354 MUSEUM MEERMANNO

Prinsessegracht 30 Voorhout ②
+31 (0)70 346 27 00
meermanno.nl

The eccentric, self-proclaimed bookworm baron van Westreenen lived in this estate, where he built an impressive library and included the book collection of his cousin Meerman. In 1852, his home opened to the public and is now considered the oldest book museum in the world. The museum also honours modern books through attractive exhibitions. In summer, the garden is a peaceful spot to read and relax.

355 LITERATUUR-MUSEUM / MUSEUM OF LITERATURE

Prins Willem-Alexanderhof 5 Stationsbuurt ②
+31 (0)70 333 96 66
literatuurmuseum.nl

The vacuum cleaner of Dutch writer Simon Vestdijk, the cigar of Louis Couperus, the motor boots of Jan Cremer: there is more to the Dutch literary heritage on display here than manuscripts alone. In addition to books of and on Dutch literary writers, the museum also showcases pictures, paintings and objects of around 6000 authors since 1750.

5

COSY THEATRES

---

356 DILIGENTIA & PEPIJN

Lange Voorhout 5
& Nieuwe School-
straat 21-23
Voorhout ②
+31 (0)70 361 05 40
diligentia-pepijn.nl

The grand podium of Diligentia and the intimate stage of PePijn together showcase all that Dutch cabaret and stand-up comedy have to offer. Diligentia has served as a theatre for over 200 years and has been updated without sacrificing its 19th-century vibe. PePijn is much smaller and younger and offers a try-out podium for new talent and seasoned comedians alike.

357 BRANOUL

Maliestraat 12
Voorhout ②
+31 (0)70 365 72 85
branoul.nl

The very small, very intimate literary theatre Branoul allows you to get up close and personal with the performers on stage. Here is where literature turns into theatre and where the wondrous world of words is the main act. Once a month, the theatre stages English-spoken stand-up comedy.

358 DE NIEUWE REGENTES

Weimarstraat 63
Segbroek ⑧
+31 (0)70 211 99 88
denieuweregentes.nl

In 1920 the largest indoor swimming pool of Europe, now a neighbourhood theatre run by a hundred volunteers bringing world-class acts on one of its four small-to-medium-sized stages. From classical music Sunday morning brunches to El Pub Flamenco evenings, there is always something going on in De Nieuwe Regentes. At this cosy theatre many remnants of the pool can still be seen.

359 KORZO

Prinsestraat 42
Hofkwartier ②
+31 (0)70 363 75 40
korzo.nl

In a former movie theatre, office building and church, Korzo offers a stage to young and talented and experimental performers from all over the world. Expect inspirational theatre plays, contemporary concerts and dynamic festivals. But above all, expect exhilarating modern dance by pioneering young choreographers.

360 THEATER AAN HET SPUI

Spui 187
Chinatown ①
+31 (0)88 356 53 56
hnt.nl

This downtown theatre is one of the three home bases for the largest travelling theatre company of the Netherlands, Het Nationale Theater. Here the company stages sharp-edge performances. Theater aan het Spui is also the scene of cutting-edge festivals, such as Movies that Matter, Holland Dance Festival and Writers Unlimited.

5 contemporary
ARTS & MOVIE CENTRES

---

361 1646 EXPERIMENTAL ART SPACE

Boekhorststraat 125
Old Centre ①
+31 (0)6 85 88 12 36
1646.nl

In the centre of The Hague, local and international artists are given a platform to reflect on current and increasingly complex social issues. The main goal of this experimental art space is to generate dialogue or to propose alternative points of view through art. The exhibitions, events and presentations are free of charge.

362 DCR

De Constant
Rebecqueplein 20-A+B
Segbroek ⑧
+31 (0)70 365 31 86
(Nest)
+31 (0)88 356 53 69
(Zaal 3)
dedcr.nl

In a former factory building complex, DCR houses artists, designers and cultural organisations, including Nest and Zaal 3. Nest is a platform for contemporary visual arts that organises exhibitions. Zaal 3 is a little theatre and part of Het Nationale Theater. The theatre gives young, emerging artists the chance to perform for an audience.

363 STROOM DEN HAAG

Hogewal 1-9
Hofkwartier ②
+31 (0)70 365 89 85
stroom.nl

Stroom is a gallery, a platform, a promotor, a library and a knowledge centre bringing together art and the urban environment. It organises cutting-edge exhibitions and lectures at its premises, art projects in the public space, and events throughout the city on art, architecture and urban planning.

364 PULCHRI STUDIO

Lange Voorhout 15
Voorhout ②
+31 (0)70 346 17 35
pulchri.nl

This association named 'out of the love for the arts' has provided a podium for predominantly Hague-based contemporary artists ever since 1847. Despite its age, it's still a relevant force in the present-day art world. In its beautiful premises, its 400+ artist members showcase their work to the public in more than 60 exhibitions per year, creating an ongoing dialogue between artists and art lovers. The works presented are for sale.

365 FILMHUIS DEN HAAG

Spui 191
Chinatown ①
+31 (0)70 365 60 30
filmhuisdenhaag.nl

In Filmhuis Den Haag, the love for film has no borders. It shows contemporary movies and classics alike, organises lectures, and hosts the renowned annual Movies that Matter Festival, a movie festival focussing on human rights and social justice.

The 5 best
ANNUAL FESTIVALS
and FAIRS

---

366 CROSSING BORDER FESTIVAL
crossingborder.nl

This festival crosses borders at many levels: between music and literature, between established and upcoming writers and performers, between countries and continents. It works, because participants on- and offstage all share one commonality: a passion for words. This festival is certain to warm and enlighten you during a grey and stormy autumn.

367 EMBASSY FESTIVAL
Lange Voorhout
Voorhout ②
+31 (0)70 360 60 33
embassyfestival.com

Despite not being the capital of the Netherlands, The Hague is where the embassies from around the globe reside. Unfortunately, these days they often hide behind heavy doors, high gates and police surveillance, but each year during one weekend in September, they set up shop at Lange Voorhout and showcase all the cultural and culinary highlights their respective countries have to offer.

368 TONG TONG FAIR
AT: MALIEVELD
Haagse Hout ② ⑥
+31 (0)70 354 09 44
tongtongfair.nl

One of the oldest and largest fairs in the Netherlands is the Tong Tong Fair, reflecting the fact that The Hague is considered the East Indies' capital of the world. The fair is primarily a podium for Indo culture so expect a wide variety of artists performing on stage and an abundance of Southeast Asian food and shopping stalls.

369 DE PARADE DEN HAAG
Westbroekpark Scheveningen – Westbroekpark ⑤
+31 (0)20 238 63 93
deparade.nl

Travelling theatre festival, medieval circus, artistic fair: the Parade is an experience you won't easily forget. Think tents in the beautiful Westbroekpark, think theatrical performances, think creative outdoor musical acts, think foods and drinks to keep you in high spirits. There is something for everyone, age and mother tongue don't matter (much).

370 WINTERNACHTEN
writersunlimited.nl

For the love for the written word! Once a year, during four days in winter, Writers Unlimited organises this international literature festival in order to connect writers and poets with each other and with scientists, artists and their audience. Many national and international well-known authors participate. It's the most important international literary event of the Netherlands.

5 great places for
LIVE MUSIC

---

371 PAARD
Prinsegracht 12
Old Centre ①
+31 (0)70 750 34 34
paard.nl

If there is one reason The Hague is still known as the City of Pop, music venue Paard it is. Annually, over 200.000 fans of pop, rock, hip-hop and dance find their way to one of Paard's three podiums. Paardcafé is for new talent and open till 4 am. Famous artists like U2, Pearl Jam and Prince performed here.

372 PODIUM DE NIEUWE KAMER
AT: VARIOUS LOCATIONS
+31 (0)6 15 52 35 72
podiumdenieuwe kamer.nl

Podium De Nieuwe Kamer is built on the foundation of the Regentenkamer, an indispensable part of the jazz scene in The Hague and breeding ground for jazz talent. It offers a virtual platform online and an actual podium at several locations throughout the city for Hague-based makers of jazz and world music.

373 RADAR CAFE BY POPRADAR
Burgemeester Hovylaan 12
Loosduinen ⑨
+31 (0)88 024 14 00
popradar.nl

Go to Radar Cafe for free concerts by young bands rooted in The Hague. Popradar is an organisation devoted to promoting popular music performed by the city's residents. It provides cheap rehearsal space, advice and a stage for new talent.

374 MURPHY'S LAW

Dr. Kuyperstraat 7
Willemspark ④
+31 (0)70 427 25 07
murphysjazz.nl

On Monday and Wednesday nights Royal Conservatoire jazz students join for jazz jam sessions to show what they have got. On Thursdays and Fridays experienced jazz musicians take the stage at this live jazz and beer cafe. Murphy's Law is the beating heart of The Hague's vibrant jazz scene.

375 MUZIEKCAFÉ DE PAAP

Papestraat 32
Hofkwartier ②
+31 (0)70 365 20 02
depaap.nl

If you can make it here, you can make it everywhere! In the past 60 years, many now-famous popular singers and bands from The Hague had there breakthroughs after late-night performances in De Paap. Come here Thursday through Saturday for live music and a drink or two... and to dance till early in the morning.

The 5 best ways to discover
INTERNATIONAL DANCE CITY THE HAGUE

---

376 HOLLAND DANCE FESTIVAL
holland-dance.com

Every two years, three weeks long, around fifty national and international dance performances in theatres throughout The Hague: the Holland Dance Festival is internationally renowned for its quality, diversity, virtuosity and creativity. From intimate performances to large-scale dance projects, from dance workshops to dance dinners: the festival always lives up to its motto: 'Dance is for everyone'.

377 CADANCE FESTIVAL
cadance.nl

New talent and leading dancers share the more intimate stages of The Hague, Korzo and Theater aan het Spui, to showcase the state of Dutch contemporary dance. Here, rising choreographers can try out new work and young dancers can show their worth. CaDance is where new dance history is in the making.

378 KORZO INDIA DANCE FESTIVAL

indiadansfestival.nl

Not just the large Hindustani community residing in The Hague shows up for the India Dance Festival. Fans come from all over the world to attend the classical and contemporary Indian dance performances. That goes for the dancers and choreographers as well, although during the festival, especially Dutch and Indian talent is on display.

379 DE DUTCH DON'T DANCE DIVISION

ddddd.nu

De Dutch Don't Dance Division was created in 1996 to accomplish exactly the opposite: to enthuse the broader public for dance. It produces multi-disciplinary dance performances for the young and the old, by amateurs and professionals. Performances are year-round, in theatres, open-air festivals, and even on the beach.

380 NDT (NEDERLANDS DANS THEATER)

ndt.nl

On the forefront of modern dance, NDT is the dance company that has put The Hague on the map as international city of contemporary dance. It started in 1959 when a group of dancers broke with the more conservative, classical ballet company Nederlands Ballet to set out in a new direction. Finding new directions has been the aim of its well-known artistic directors, such as Van Manen, Kylián and Lightfoot, till this day.

The 5 best places to spot
STREET ART *and*
MURALS

---

381 SWEELINCKPLEIN
**Scheveningen –
Duinoord** ③

That street art can embellish a neighbourhood does proof the *trompe-l'oeil* on a small dreary electricity building situated on the Sweelinckplein, a square with a lush green park and stately houses. Artist Jille van der Veen, specialised in realistic art that deceives the eye, turned this concrete box into a lovely garden house. In summer, the wall painting blends into the park surrounding it.

382 WEGASTRAAT

382 WEGASTRAAT

Wegastraat 67
Laak ⑦

The large electricity building at the industrial zone the Binckhorst got a facelift with two eye-catching works of street art. The front mural by Karski & Beyond refers to the past and present of the Binckhorst. The side mural by Lily Brik depicts St Barbara, the name-giver of the nearby cemetery.

383 CEMETERY ST BARBARA

Sint Barbaraweg 6
Laak ⑦
+31 (0)70 350 37 18
begraafplaats
stbarbara.nl

In the middle of the rough and industrial Binckhorst area, this Roman Catholic cemetery is a welcome oasis of peace. At the modern oratory in the transparent chapel, street artist Patrick Artdrenaline was commissioned to make a beautiful black and white mural.

384 MURALS AT SCHEVENINGEN

Heemraadstraat,
Marcelisstraat,
Badhuisstraat,
Jan Kistenstraat
Scheveningen

Wandering through the back streets of Scheveningen, you may stumble upon several life-size murals by Kees van der Vlies. Some of the murals depict Scheveningen around 1900 and remind of the Dutch painter Hendrik Willem Mesdag, who painted his famous panorama at the nearby Seinpostduin in 1881.

385 WALL POEMS

Archipel and
Willemspark
archipelpoezie.nl

Poems by Dutch and international poets grace the walls of residential buildings in the Archipel and Willemspark neighbourhoods. Works by Dutch poets like Vasalis and Rutger Kopland, as well as American poets like William Carlos Williams and Emily Dickinson invite you to slow down and contemplate.

5 remarkable
PIECES OF MODERN PUBLIC ART

---

386 ZIEKEN TE BED
BY JAN SNOECK
Lijnbaan 32
Old Centre ①

Trained at the Royal Academy of Art in The Hague, Jan Snoeck is known for his abstract and monumental ceramic sculptures. *Zieken te bed* behind the Westeinde hospital, is a terrific example: laying down or sitting up, ten colourful patients occupy as many light blue beds.

387 DE TERP VAN LEIDSCHENVEEN / THE MOUND OF LEIDSCHENVEEN
Vrouw Avenweg, Molenpolderstraat
Leidschenveen-Ypenburg ⑦

Post a picture of this lonely church on top of a mound and your followers will think you are in Tirol. However, this church stands on top of a covered garbage dump. The mound and church are a work of art by Laurens Kolks and Dennis Lohuis. It's a fine example of optical illusion since the church is teeny-weeny and the mound only 11 metres high.

388 PARK IN HET WATER
Laakhaven
Laak ⑦

Opposite The Hague School of Applied Sciences, the New York based Vito Acconci & Studio created a slightly tilted park that seems to have broken off its surroundings. Together they look like pieces of a puzzle, with water of the Laakhaven running in between.

389 HEMELS GEWELF / CELESTIAL VAULT
Machiel
Vrijenhoeklaan 175
Loosduinen ⑨

At first, it might feel a bit weird to lie down on the stone bench in the middle of a large artificial crater in the dunes of Kijkduin. But once you observe how the sky becomes a vault, you get this magically serene feeling. The effect is most noticeable on clear days. This public art work is created by the American artist James Turrell, the artist of light and space.

390 DE BEELDENGALERIJ
Grote Marktstraat,
Spui, Kalvermarkt
Old Centre

Since the nineties 40 oval pedestals in the shopping district near the city hall have carried as many sculptures by present-day Dutch or Netherlands-based artists. Every now and then, the movable sculptures trade places or are replaced by new additions keeping passers-by fresh and current on Dutch contemporary art.

387 DE TERP VAN LEIDSCHENVEEN / THE MOUND OF LEIDSCHENVEEN

SKATEPARK DE KUIL

30 THINGS TO DO
WITH CHILDREN

———————

5 cool **PLAYGROUNDS** and **SKATEPARKS** —— 210

The 5 best shops for **TOYS** and **BOOKS** ———— 212

5 lovely shops for **CHILDREN'S CLOTHING** —— 214

The 5 best **MUSEUMS FOR KIDS** ————— 216

5 great **ACTIVITIES FOR KIDS** ————— 218

The 5 best places to **EAT WITH KIDS** ———— 220

5 cool
PLAYGROUNDS *and*
SKATEPARKS

---

391 SKATEPARK SWEATSHOP

Binckhorstlaan 271
Laak ⑦
+31 (0)70 752 34 11
skateparksweatshop.nl

This unpolished indoor skatepark in the Binckhorst industrial park is for beginners as well as the more advanced. Younger kids can have a skateboard party here, lessons included. And what to think of a cool skateboard-graffiti party? After 6 pm, this skatepark is taken over by the older and more experienced skateboarders.

392 SKATEPARK DE KUIL & ZANDSPEELTUIN

Ary van der Spuyweg 1
Scheveningen – Scheveningse Bosjes ③⑤

This place is fun for kids of all ages. At the skatepark teenagers can practise their skateboarding skills, in the adjacent playground younger kids can enjoy themselves with slides, aerial walkways, ramps and ladders. The playground is well kept and clean. It's built on sand and secluded by trees of the Scheveningse Bosjes.

393 **HET APENBOS**
AT: BOSJES VAN POOT
Laan van Poot 93
Segbroek ⑧

Kids of the adjacent school and scouting club helped to design this playground in a small forest in the Vogelwijk. In addition to equipment for swinging, balancing and clambering, they asked for a zip wire and enough space to play soccer. The wooden playing equipment adds to the green look and feel.

394 **MONKEYBOS**
AT: MEIJENDEL
Meijendelseweg 40
Wassenaar –
Suburbs North ⑥
dunea.nl

Meijendel is a wonderful large dune area between The Hague and Wassenaar. In the middle of this nature reserve, next to the visitors centre, you will find this large natural playground. Kids can act like monkeys, climbing trees or crawling through massive water pipes. There is also a zip wire, a lookout tower, and much more.

395 **PLANET JUMP**
Stadhouders-
plantsoen 28
Scheveningen –
Zorgvliet ③
+31 (0)70 779 61 80
planetjump.nl

On rainy days, this indoor trampoline park is a kids' paradise. The entire floor of the former church is covered with trampolines. For younger jumpers there is a separate area on the balcony. An obstacle course and a climbing wall add to the adventure. To assure safety, the number of jumpers is limited.

The 5 best shops for
TOYS and BOOKS

396 ROOD MET WITTE STIPPEN

Beeklaan 303
Segbroek ⑧
+31 (0)70 346 39 48
roodmetwittestippen.nl

This must be the most beautiful little toyshop in town. It's situated in a former monumental De Gruyter shop (until the 1970s, a famous Dutch grocer) with art deco details and original tile panels. The owners, Karin and Rien, handpick all toys and handicrafts they sell.

397 DE KIKKERKONING

Aert van der Goesstraat 48
Scheveningen – Statenkwartier ③
+31 (0)70 351 42 27
dekikkerkoning denhaag.nl

It's hard to leave this enchanting shop without a present. It's packed with all sorts of beautiful (baby) toys, soft stuffed animals, children's books, board games and puzzles. In addition to toys, this shop sells adorable children's clothing. It also has attractive items for moms, like purses, baskets and wallets.

398 ALICE IN WONDERLAND

Piet Heinstraat 2
Zeeheldenkwartier ④
+31 (0)70 310 69 92
dehaagsekinder boekenwinkel.nl

This is how a children's bookshop should be. Alice in Wonderland is inviting and has a knowledgeable staff. It has a wide range of Dutch and some English books, from books for babies and toddlers to books for young adults. The bookshop regularly organises events, such as small performances and book signings.

399 MATRUSCHKA
Van Hoytema-
straat 57
Haagse Hout ⑥
+31 (0)70 360 52 18
matruschka.nl

Toys made of wood and other natural materials, dolls, books, school supplies, art supplies, children's lighting, adorable costumes, and organic and natural kids' clothing. Matruschka is much more than a toyshop! This lovely shop has been around for decades (albeit on a different location) and is still a local favourite.

400 HOUT SAGE SPEELGOED
Molenstraat 21-C
Hofkwartier ②
+31 (0)6 57 99 40 39
houtsagespeelgoed.nl

This shop specialises in toys made from wood. Wooden toys are not only beautiful and fun to play with, they are also timeless and last for generations. The owner is very passionate about his products and makes sure they are made of sustainable wood. Babies, toddlers and older kids: Hout Sage has toys for every age.

396 ROOD MET WITTE STIPPEN

5 lovely shops for
CHILDREN'S CLOTHING

---

401 **ELVIS & OTIS**
Prins Hendrik-
straat 124
Zeeheldenkwartier ③
+31 (0)70 752 03 58
elvisandotis.com

A little shop for hip kids and cool parents. Elvis & Otis, named after the kids of the owner, sells high-quality brands, like MarMar Copenhagen, Repose AMS, Tinycottons and I Dig Denim. At this delightful shop you'll also find imaginative toys and gifts, like the funny and super soft stuffed animals by Jellycat.

402 **LITTLEYOU**

402 LITTLEYOU

Boreelstraat 8
Scheveningen –
Statenkwartier ③
+31 (0)6 81 05 02 28
littleyou.me

A most charming little concept store for kids. Young kids can enjoy themselves in the fun play corner while parents shop or drink coffee or tea. The congenial owner Julia Bos sells sustainable high-quality children's clothing by Scandinavian and German brands, as well as beautiful toys and nursery and interior design items.

403 ACHTUNG! BABY

Prins Hendrik-
straat 97
Zeeheldenkwartier ③
+31 (0)70 737 13 06
achtung-baby.nl

What a great idea to sell secondhand kids' clothing! The owners, Ginny and Maryke, only accept quality brands and clothes that are clean and still in good condition. Besides clothes, you'll find adorable handmade gifts here.

404 PLUK & PALOMA

2e Schuytstraat 168
Scheveningen –
Duinoord ③
+31 (0)70 369 79 05
plukandpaloma.com

Just around the corner of the Reinken-straat you'll find this lovely shop of Anca Huizenga. The shop is jammed with colourful kids' clothing, small and high-quality brands like Wynken and Maed for mini. Anca also sells toys and books, and beautiful jewellery for the moms.

405 STOKSTAART

Weimarstraat 65
Segbroek ⑧
+31 (0)6 45 23 00 45
stokstaartshop.nl

Comfortable and sustainable clothing, accessories, toys and books for kids aged 0-12 years. Think soft and playful fabrics by CarlijnQ, handmade wooden toys by Raduga Grez, cool cardboard creations by Studio ROOF. Small brands that are fair trade and ethical. They also sell beautiful work from children's book illustrators.

The 5 best
MUSEUMS FOR KIDS

---

406 MUSEON

Stadhouderslaan 37
Scheveningen –
Zorgvliet ③
+31 (0)70 338 13 38
museon.nl

This museum for culture and science is entertaining for the whole family. The themes of the permanent and temporary exhibitions are highly educational, yet kids won't get bored. They learn by playing, looking, listening and reading: the exhibitions are interactive by design. The central exhibition, One Planet, covers the hot topic of how to keep the earth liveable.

407 KINDERBOEKEN-MUSEUM

Prins Willem-
Alexanderhof 5
Stationsbuurt ②
+31 (0)70 333 96 66
*kinderboeken
museum.nl*

A fun and interactive museum where kids can use their imagination and lose themselves in their favourite book and playfully become part of it. There are two departments: one for the younger kids (age 2 to 6) and one for the older ones (age 7+). The expositions are based on Dutch children's books.

408 BEELD EN GELUID DEN HAAG

Zeestraat 82
Zeeheldenkwartier ④
+31 (0)70 330 75 00
comm.nl

How do we communicate nowadays? How did we communicate in the past? What is non-verbal communication? Can we imagine a world without the internet? At this highly interactive and recently renovated museum, kids can discover everything there is to know about communication. 'He who understands the art of communication, understands the world', is their motto.

409 CHAMBERS OF WONDER

AT: KUNSTMUSEUM
DEN HAAG
Stadhouderslaan 41
Scheveningen –
Zorgvliet ③
+31 (0)70 338 11 11
kunstmuseum.nl

In the basement of the Kunstmuseum, formerly known as the Gemeente- museum, there is a permanent inspiring and fun department for kids and parents. In the Chambers of Wonder, thirteen beautifully decorated rooms, children can become museum director for a day. With the aid of a tablet they design an exhibition and along their journey they complete exciting challenges.

410 ESCHER IN THE PALACE

AT: LANGE VOORHOUT
PALACE
Lange Voorhout 74
Voorhout ②
+31 (0)70 427 77 30
escherinhetpaleis.nl

The work of the world-famous artist M.C. Escher is very interesting for somewhat older kids. Escher, the master of optical illusion, liked to fool the spectator and to provoke the sense of wonder that kids love. In an interactive permanent exhibition on the second floor, visitors can become part of Escher's wondrous world.

5 great
ACTIVITIES FOR KIDS

411 OMNIVERSUM
President
Kennedylaan 5
Scheveningen –
Zorgvliet ③
+31 (0)70 354 54 54
omniversum.nl

Kids love this cinema! The huge dome-shaped screen of the Omniversum lets you become part of the movie, which is quite a stunning experience. Most shows are educational movies about space and wildlife and last about an hour.

412 HAAGSE BOOMTOPPERS
AT: VARIOUS LOCATIONS
+31 (0)6 42 20 98 09
haagseboomtoppers.nl

This recreational tree climbing event is a fun and safe activity for kids aged seven and over. The skilled instructors set up the climbing equipment in a park and supervise the kids. It's both possible to join an organised climbing session (check Facebook) or to book a children's party.

413 KOOMAN'S POPPENTHEATER
Frankenstraat 66
Scheveningen –
Statenkwartier ③
+31 (0)70 355 93 05
koomans poppentheater.nl

This charming puppet theatre has been around since 1960. It's a magical place where beautiful puppets come to life. The owner, Arjan Kooman, creates everything himself: the puppets, the decors and the stories. His brother Joost Kooman composes the music. The performances are aimed at children aged 5 and up. In Dutch only.

414 AVONTURIA DE VOGELKELDER

Kerketuinenweg 3
Escamp ⑨
+31 (0)70 363 72 72
de-vogelkelder.nl

This enormous pet shop (the largest in the Netherlands!) is also a mini theme park with many activities for kids. Let them feel like Indiana Jones in the mini zoo with dark caves, a temple, reptiles, spiders and bats. You can also throw your kids' birthday party here and let them do adventurous things like gold digging, holding a snake and even eating insects.

415 DE JUTTERSKEET

BEHIND HOTEL ATLANTIC
Loosduinen ⑨
jutterskeet.nl

The Hague has its own beach comber: Ome Jan (Uncle John). On Saturday and Sunday afternoon you can find him and his assistant Rob in a little shed filled with interesting finds close to Kijkduin Beach. Ome Jan is happy to teach you how to become a real beach comber yourself. You can hire a metal detector or a fishing net here.

414 AVONTURIA DE VOGELKELDER

The 5 best places to
EAT WITH KIDS

---

416 VILLA OCKENBURGH – DE KAS

Monsterseweg 4
Loosduinen ⑨
+31 (0)70 217 73 33
villaockenburgh.nl

The almost four-centuries-old estate in the beautiful and green Park Ockenburgh has recently been fully renovated. The restaurant in the villa is for the parents, but the greenhouse is for everyone. Have the kids participate in the many activities organised there or pick up a healthy lunch and take them for an adventurous walk through the woods, waterways, meadows and dunes of the Park.

417 OMA TOOS

Dr. Lelykade 3-R
Scheveningen –
Harbour ⑤
+31 (0)70 444 94 28
oma-toos.nl

When visiting Holland with kids you must eat Dutch *poffertjes* and pancakes at least once. Oma Toos, overlooking the harbour of Scheveningen, is specialised in Dutch food and has many special pancakes and *poffertjes* on the menu, even savoury ones. The restaurant is very child-friendly with a play corner and a kind, patient staff.

418 DE BOOM-HUTTENCLUB

Boekhorststraat 47
Old Centre ①
deboomhuttenclub.nl

To give the somewhat neglected Boekhorststraat in the centre a boost, this sustainable restaurant annex indoor playground in a former cinema was created. A unique place and brilliant concept where parents can have a healthy lunch and a great coffee, while their little ones enjoy themselves in the playground made of wood.

419 PLUK! DEN HAAG

Loosduinse Hoofd-
straat 1184-A
Loosduinen ⑨
plukdenhaag.nl

This city farm on the edge of town is a great place to relax for parents with young kids. In addition to a large organic vegetable garden where you can pick your own veggies, it boasts a petting zoo and a small natural playground. Have lunch here on the terrace while your kids are having fun on the property.

420 DE WATERKANT

AT: WESTBROEKPARK
Scheveningen –
Westbroekpark ⑤
+31 (0)70 350 28 63
dewaterkant.nl

Rent a rowing boat, have a cup of tea and a childproof lunch, and relax. The lush waterside terrace of De Waterkant is a wonderful location to go to with somewhat older kids. You can reach this open-air cafe through the Westbroekpark or take the little pedestrian ferry from the Haringkade. Open in spring and summer.

20 PLACES
TO SLEEP

The 5 best boutique HOTELS *and* B&Bs ———————— 224

5 UNUSUAL PLACES *to sleep* ———————————— 226

5 COOL *and* CHEAP *places to stay*———————— 228

5 hotels in REMARKABLE BUILDINGS ———————— 230

The 5 best boutique
HOTELS *and* B&Bs

421 RESIDENZ STADSLOGEMENT

Sweelinckplein 35
Scheveningen –
Duinoord ③
+31 (0)70 364 61 90
residenz.nl

If there is one place in the city that truly is 'home away from home', Residenz Stadslogement it is. Petra and Frank personally welcome you to one of the six classy suites and apartments in their home, situated at the beautiful neo-Renaissance style square Sweelinckplein. It might even be better than home, since they serve you a fresh and copious breakfast every day.

421 RESIDENZ STADSLOGEMENT

422 LA PAULOWNA

Anna Paulowna-
plein 3
Zeeheldenkwartier ④
+31 (0)70 450 00 91
lapaulowna.com

Spacious, airy and bright, ecological and sustainable, moderately priced, situated at the lively Anna Paulownaplein: this boutique hotel has a lot going for it. Its owners lived across the street, when they fell for this end-of-the-19th-century building, so they know how to make you feel at home in this classy part of town.

423 STADSVILLA MOZAIC

Laan Copes van
Cattenburch 38
Archipel ④
+31 (0)70 352 23 35
mozaic.nl

In 1880, the city's elites drove their horses and carriages through this posh part of town. Today, the grandeur of the Archipel neighbourhood has not faded. Experience contemporary comfort and modern design in this 140-years-old mansion. Parks, beaches and the city centre are all a stone's throw away.

424 HOTEL PISTACHE

Scheveningseweg 1
Archipel ④
+31 (0)6 15 21 69 41
hotelpistache.nl

Two interior designers started this boutique hotel in an art deco building across from the Peace Palace. Hotel Pistache is no standard hotel: it offers individually designed suites that make you feel right at home.

425 BACÁN B&B

Molenstraat 39-A
Hofkwartier ②
+31 (0)6 34 14 41 35
bacan.nl

Be the King's neighbour in one of two royal suites in Molenstraat, one of the oldest streets in The Hague. Even if royal proximity has no particular appeal to you, this B&B has much to offer. The suites are stylish and luxurious. The neighbourhood Hofkwartier (Court's Quarter) has some of the best shops, bars and restaurants in town.

5

UNUSUAL PLACES
to sleep

---

426 **DE PIER, SUITES & CABINS**

Strandweg 152
Scheveningen –
Beach ⑤
+31 (0)6 10 72 04 38
piersuites.nl

Ever since its opening in 1961, De Pier has reinvented itself over and over. One of the latest additions is De Pier, Suites & Cabins: the first place in the Netherlands where you can sleep over the North Sea. The suites are equipped with a Jacuzzi and glass ceilings allowing for star gazing.

427 **HAAGSE STRANDHUISJES / BEACH HOUSES**

Strandslag 2-A
Loosduinen ⑨
haagsestrandhuisjes.nl

Listen to the seagulls squawking, the waves breaking, the wind blowing through the reeds. See the sun rise over the dunes and set over the horizon. Be the first and the last on the beach when sleeping in one of the twenty remote Kijkduin beach houses.

428 **SLAPEN OP DE BOOT / SLEEPING ON THE BOAT**

Wateringseweg 95
Poeldijk –
Suburbs South ⑨
+31 (0)6 14 15 82 51
slapenopdeboot.nl

Amidst the greenhouses of the Westland, this charming B&B boat is perfect if you want to escape the hustle and bustle of the city. The small boat has two clean bedrooms, a kitchenette, plus a shower cabin and private terrace on shore. Although you cannot take the boat on a trip, it is possible to fish, swim, or explore the surroundings by canoe.

429 KASTEEL DE WITTENBURG

Landgoed de
Wittenburg 1
Wassenaar –
Suburbs North ⑥
+31 (0)70 515 15 00
wittenburg.nl

A monumental farmhouse around 1600, built into a castle-like mansion in 1899, transformed into the hotel it is today: this Wassenaar estate has seen many changes over the past centuries. Sleep in one of its ten exclusive castle rooms and suites and spend the night in the quietest and most upscale suburb of The Hague.

430 THE GARDEN HOUSE

AT: HOF VAN WOUW
Brouwersgracht 30
Old Centre ①
hofvanwouw.nl

The tiny houses in this 1647 residential courtyard are only available for the extended stay of single women with limited means. There is one exception: the Garden House is slightly larger and available for couples as a B&B, offering a unique opportunity to experience life in an environment where over the centuries little has changed.

427 HAAGSE STRANDHUISJES / BEACH HOUSES

5
COOL *and* CHEAP

places to stay

---

431 KINGKOOL

Prinsegracht 51
Old Centre ①
+31 (0)70 215 83 39
kingkool.nl

With both mixed dorms for backpackers, a bunny dorm for boys only and private rooms for families, KingKool is an affordable place to sleep for anyone visiting The Hague. And just as its name suggests: it's very cool thanks to the different themes and designs throughout the hostel. It has a bar where you can play chess, pool and ping-pong. And buy designer sneakers on top.

432 JORPLACE BEACH HOSTEL

Keizerstraat 296
Scheveningen –
Beach ⑤
+31 (0)70 338 32 70
jorplace.nl

The ultimate place to sleep for young surf loving digital nomads… and everyone else. Jorplace offers bunkbed group accommodation and rooms for two in the main street of old Scheveningen village. It has a very relaxed vibe, the bar doesn't close (until it does), you can hang out around a fire, and even cook your own meal.

433 HOSTEL THE HAGUE

Lutherse Burgwal 5
Old Centre ①
+31 (0)70 220 40 26
hostelthehague.com

This small hostel with basic rooms is smack in the middle of the liveliest part of town, close to where the night life is. However, there is no need to go anywhere: the hostel bar has craft beer on tap and in bottles, and live jazz music almost every night. Just make sure to be under 40 and a sound sleeper.

434 THE STUDENT HOTEL

Hoefkade 9
Stationsbuurt ①
+31 (0)70 762 10 00
thestudenthotel.com

Whether you're still in school, young or old, a traveller, or a professional nomad, at The Student Hotel you can explore your inner-student. The hotel offers short-stay rooms and long-stay apartments, plus an abundance of co-studying, co-living, co-working and co-relaxing spaces. Hip to the core, as centrally located as it gets, and affordable no less.

435 TELEPORT HOTEL

Binckhorstlaan 131
Laak ⑦
+31 (0)70 204 40 22
thehague.
teleporthotel.com

The location in the heart of the industrial Binckhorst is far from romantic. But inside, the hotel has cool vibes: the spacious lobby has giant street art pieces painted on its walls. The rooms are bright, modern and offer great views. Try to book one of the street art rooms. The Hague is working hard to transform the Binckhorst into a hip area. Soon, this hotel might be in the middle of where it all happens.

5 hotels in
REMARKABLE BUILDINGS

---

436 CARLTON AMBASSADOR

Sophialaan 2
Willemspark ④
+31 (0)70 363 03 63
carlton.nl

Experience chic The Hague at this high-end hotel in a stately, historical white building. The large hotel is surrounded by trees and embassies, and is very close to the Peace Palace and Panorama Mesdag. The rooms and suites are richly decorated with flower patterns and delftware touches.

437 STAYBRIDGE SUITES THE HAGUE – PARLIAMENT

Lange Vijverberg 10
Voorhout ②
+31 (0)70 209 90 30
staybridge.com

The location of this hotel opposite the historical parliament buildings is unique. The 101 luxurious modern suites with fully equipped kitchens are divided over two historical buildings with spectacular views over the Court Pond and a modern building in the back. Ideal for families and extended stays.

438 COVE CENTRUM

Grote Marktstraat 46
Old Centre ①
staycove.com

Ultra-modern, with cool urban vibes, and in the heart of the shopping district. The white building with large black round windows is like a giant spotted cow. The large lounge feels like a living room, with free coffee and game boards at hand. The rooms and suites are basic but clean and well equipped.

439 IBIS STYLES CITY CENTRE

Kerkplein 3
Old Centre ①
+31 (0)70 216 19 58
accorhotels.com

Impressive brickwork, stained glass, nature stone details and a spectacular staircase: this affordable hotel occupies a historical building designed by the famous Dutch architect Berlage. The location in the heart of the city and opposite the centuries-old church is terrific, but it can get a bit noisy when the bells start ringing.

440 HOTEL INDIGO THE HAGUE-PALACE NOORDEINDE

Noordeinde 33
Hofkwartier ②
+31 (0)70 209 90 00
ihg.com

Opposite Noordeinde Palace and located in a historical bank building, this place has more to offer than just a good night's rest. The hotel with marble walls, high ceilings, stained glass and stylish rooms is both luxurious and cosy. The restaurant is situated where the cash-out area used to be, the cocktail bar is tucked away in the former gold vault: a must-visit.

439 IBIS STYLES CITY CENTRE

BEACH SPORTS

45 ACTIVITIES FOR WEEKENDS

The 5 best **BOAT TRIPS** —————————— 234

5 great places to **PRACTISE BEACH SPORTS**
and **BEACH YOGA** —————————— 236

5 special places to **SWIM OUTDOORS** ————— 238

The 5 best **GUIDED TOURS** ———————— 240

The 5 best **BIKE TOURS** ———————— 242

5 exceptional places to **EXPLORE NATURE** ——— 244

5 interesting ways to explore **THE WESTLAND** — 246

5 great places to **RELAX** and **UNWIND**———— 248

The 5 most inspiring **THINGS TO LEARN** ——— 250

The 5 best
BOAT TRIPS

---

441 OOIEVAART

Bierkade 18-B
Chinatown ①
+31 (0)70 445 18 69
ooievaart.nl

Ooievaart, run by volunteers, offers various boat tours from spring to autumn. Enjoy, for example, a royal tour, a Van Gogh tour or a celebrity tour. The excursions are in open boats and the knowledgeable volunteers will tell you juicy stories and reveal the city's secrets. There are English-spoken trips every day at 3 pm.

442 REDERIJ VROLIJK

Dr. Lelykade 3-H
Scheveningen –
Harbour ⑤
+31 (0)70 351 40 21
rederijvrolijk.com

Catching fish at sea! How cool is that? This shipping company in Scheveningen offers various sportfishing cruises throughout the year. Mackerel, whiting, plaice, codfish: with a little bit of luck you'll bring these fish ashore. In winter, wreck fishing is also an option. And if you are not into fishing at all: this company offers standard boat cruises along the Dutch coast as well.

443 THE HAGUE BOAT

PICK-UP AND DROP-OFF:
Mauritskade 10
Willemspark ④
+31 (0)6 39 82 35 46
thehagueboat.com

Bring your friends and family and enjoy a cheerful boat cruise at The Hague Boat. Regular boat tours as well as special excursions can be booked here. While travelling through the tranquil canals of The Hague, you can indulge a high tea, a brunch, or a refreshing glass of prosecco with small bites.

444 WILLEMSVAART

VARIOUS PICK-UP
LOCATIONS
City Centre
Scheveningen
+31 (0)6 19 85 32 80
willemsvaart.nl

A fun way to start your day at Scheveningen Beach is to go there by boat. Willemsvaart offers one-way trips to the beach through the Canal that runs from The Hague Central Station to the Haringkade. You'll pass busy city streets as well as the lush and silent Westbroekpark. Willemsvaart also organises group tours and tours during special events and festivals, like Prince's day and Sail Scheveningen.

445 KANOVERHUUR DEN HAAG / CANOE RENTAL

BOAT OPPOSITE:
Groenewegje 144
Stationsbuurt ①
+31 (0)6 85 11 88 22
kanoverhuur
denhaag.nl

It's possible to explore The Hague by canoe! Rent a canoe at Kanoverhuur and glide through the canals of the city. Admire the buildings, modern architecture and city parks from the water, and take a break at one of the many canal-side cafes. Kanoverhuur offers several fun and diverse canoe routes.

5 great places to
PRACTISE BEACH SPORTS
and BEACH YOGA

---

446 HART BEACH SURF SCHOOL

Strandweg 3-B
Scheveningen –
Beach ⑤
+31 (0)70 350 25 91
hartbeach.nl

Always wanted to learn how to ride the waves? This school offers year-round professional surf instruction, for kids, beginners, and surf experts eager to pick up a few new moves. Besides surfing lessons, it's also possible to attend SUP and skateboard lessons. Hart Beach also has a relaxed beach pavilion on the beach and a cool surf shop in the harbour.

447 THE HAGUE BEACH STADIUM

Strandweg 4
Scheveningen –
Beach ⑤
+31 (0)70 762 02 76
beachstadium.com

Practising sports on the beach in your bikini or swimming shorts, at The Hague Beach Stadium sports fans of all levels can get active. Whether you play a game of beach volleyball or beach soccer with a group of friends, or attend one of the many sports events, being outdoors on the beach will give you an amazing energy boost.

448 BLOW! KITESURFING SCHOOL

Zandmotorpad
(7-minute walk from
Parking at Machiel
Vrijenhoeklaan)
Loosduinen ⑨
+31 (0)6 52 53 49 99
blow.surf

The location of this fun kitesurf school, close to De Zandmotor, a manmade peninsula on the coast near Kijkduin, is ideal. This quiet, shallow, flat water spot with a steady sea breeze is perfect for both beginners and the more advanced. At the relaxed beach house, you can change, shower, and have a drink and a bite after a kitesurf session.

449 YOGA ON THE BEACH

VARIOUS LOCATIONS
Loosduinen
Scheveningen

Sand forces you to keep your balance and to use muscles you might not be using on the yoga mat. During summer, many yoga schools in town offer yoga classes on the sandy beaches of The Hague. And many beach pavilions have a separate space for yoga if the weather is bad. Beach yoga can be practised at, for example, Pier 32, Patagonia Beach, Strandtent 14 and Het Puntje. Check yoga school websites and *buiten-yoga.nl* for locations and times.

450 THE SHORE

Strandweg 2-A
Scheveningen –
Beach ⑤
+31 (0)6 49 39 20 95
theshore.nl

The most laidback surfing school at the Dutch coast! It doesn't just offer professional surfing lessons, taught by skilled instructors, but it is a great place to hang out as well. The organic juices, pancakes and speciality beers are a welcome treat after an intense surfing session. This school has a deep connection with the environment and takes sustainability very seriously.

5 special places to
SWIM OUTDOORS

---

451 MADESTEIN RECREATIONAL PARK

Several entrances at Madepolderweg
Loosduinen ⑨

The North Sea is not the only place to take a refreshing swim. On the edge of The Hague, near Kijkduin, is Park Madestein. A large park where you'll find two recreational lakes with a number of small beaches and playing areas.

452 ZWEMBAD DE PUT

Huis te
Landelaan 29-A
Rijswijk –
Suburbs South ⑨
+31 (0)70 390 47 29
zwembaddeput.nl

Take a dive in a natural pool! This piece of nature in Rijswijk, just outside The Hague, is a true gem. Hidden behind apartment buildings you'll find the green and historical estate Te Werve with a natural pool in a manmade lake that dates back to 1910.

453 WASSENAARSE SLAG

De Wassenaarse
Slag 31
Wassenaar –
Suburbs North

If you like to combine a hiking or cycling tour with a refreshing dive in the North Sea, a visit to the sandy beach of Wassenaar is just for you. To reach this beach you pass through Meijendel, a beautiful nature reserve with a wide dune landscape, forests and lakes. During summer, you can have drinks and dinner at several beach pavilions.

454 VLIETLAND

Suburbs North
*recreatiegebied-
vlietland.nl*

This large recreational area in between The Hague and Leiden has everything in store for a fun and family-friendly water day. With three lakes, many beaches and all sorts of water sports facilities, like sailing, canoeing and rowing, this is a popular place to relax. For kids, there is a floating Aquapark as well.

455 NUDIST BEACHES

Strandslag 1,
Strandslag 8,
Scheveningen
Northern Beach
Scheveningen –
Beach / Loosduinen
*strand-denhaag.nl/
overzicht/naaktstranden*

Although still taboo in many places around the world, The Hague has no less than three nudist beaches. Two at the Southern Beach and one at the Northern Beach, near Scheveningen. No need to get thirsty or hungry on these somewhat remote and quiet beaches, because they all have beach pavilions nearby. Do not forget to bring your sunblock, though!

451 MADESTEIN RECREATIONAL PARK

The 5 best
GUIDED TOURS

456 KURHAUS WITH HIGH TEA

Gevers Deynoot-
plein 30
Scheveningen –
Beach ⑤
+31 (0)70 416 26 36
*amrathkurhaus.com/
en/grand-tour.html*

Get to know everything about the turbulent history of this iconic hotel: which celebrities stayed and performed here, what happened with the building during the German occupation? Learn about the fire, the decay in the 1970s and, fortunately, the subsequent restoration of the building. A guided tour includes a visit to the special dome high up in the hotel and a high tea afterwards.

457 SCULPTURE GARDEN CLINGENBOSCH

Dennenlaan 9
Wassenaar –
Suburbs North ⑥
+31 (0)70 512 16 60
voorlinden.nl

If you are impressed by Museum Voorlinden, which houses the private collection of art collector Joop van Caldenborgh, this sculpture garden at the 27-hectare property of Caldenborgh's private estate Clingenbosch is also a must. A two-hour guided tour is available on Thursdays from 3 to 6 pm (from May until October). Henry Moore, Jean Tinguely, Sylvie Fleury, Sol LeWitt can all be admired here.

458 VISAFSLAG SCHEVENINGEN / FISH AUCTION

Visafslagweg 1
Scheveningen –
Harbour ⑤
+31 (0)70 361 88 60
vvv.nl

Drag yourself out of bed, get a glimpse of the life of the hardworking fishermen and see the fish auction at Scheveningen harbour in action. Which fish are on sale, how does an auction work, what makes Scheveningen so special? The tour starts as early as 6.30 am, but you will be welcomed with a hot cup of coffee to wake you up.

459 PRODEMOS

Hofweg 1
Voorhout ②
+31 (0)70 757 02 00
prodemos.nl

For anyone who is curious about how Dutch democracy works, this 'House for Democracy and the Rule of Law' is the place to book a tour. Right across from the Binnenhof, the centre of political life, Prodemos offers several guided tours to the Dutch House of Representatives, the Senate and the Hall of Knights. The historical buildings at the Binnenhof have quite a few intriguing stories to tell.

460 ROYAL WAITING ROOM

AT: TRAIN STATION
DEN HAAG HS
Stationsplein 41
Stationsbuurt ①
artifex.nu/
wachtkamers

Times have changed, but the Royal Waiting Room from 1893, at train station Hollands Spoor, is still in use by the Royal Family on the rare occasion when travelling by train is more convenient than travelling by plane or automobile. The extravagant waiting rooms above the main station hall can be visited under guidance. Visitors will be surprised by the size and the splendour.

The 5 best
BIKE TOURS

461 ATLANTIKWALL BIKE TOUR
Bike route number 158310
route.nl

Many remnants of the Atlantic Wall, an extensive system of coastal defence built by Nazi Germany during World War II, can still be seen in and around The Hague. During this tour, you pass bunkers, the lost Jewish quarter and the place where the yearly commemoration of the victims is held. This self-guided tour is 34 km long and can be navigated by following intersection numbers (check the website).

462 CYCLE TOUR CASTLE DUIVENVOORDE
fietsnetwerk.nl

Get on your bike and explore the green surroundings of The Hague. You'll pass castles and estates in Wassenaar, Voorschoten and Voorburg, built centuries ago by the nobility and wealthy merchants. There are several great options for lunch or a drink, for example at the modern tea pavilion Hof van Duivenvoorde. This self-guided tour in English can be navigated by following intersection numbers (check the website).

463 THE HAGUE BIKE TOURS

STARTS AT:

Heulstraat 13
Hofkwartier ②
+31 (0)70 313 44 00
thehaguebiketours.nl

Brent Meelhuysen was only thirteen years old when he started this successful bike tour company in 2017. Expect a well-organised and lively bike tour with an experienced guide – sometimes it's Brent, sometimes a colleague – through the city centre. Highlights, secret places, interesting stories and a typical pastry of The Hague are included. A must do!

464 MUSEUM BIKE TOUR BY HAAGSCHE STADSFIETS

AT: DU-NORD RIJWIELEN

Keizerstraat 27-29
Scheveningen –
Old Town ⑤
+31 (0)70 355 40 60
fietsverhuur
zuidholland.nl

Rent a museum bike and enjoy a self-guided tour along the museums of your choice. Upon presenting your museum bike key to the museums, you'll receive a little surprise. With the rent of the museum bike come a booklet (also available in English) and a handy map. If you do not feel like museum hopping, the booklet also offers a beautiful dune route.

465 CYCLE AND THE CITY

Halstraat 12
Hofkwartier ②
+31 (0)6 24 46 71 55
cycleandthecity.nl

This tour is gold! Discover the highlights and secrets of downtown The Hague on a golden bike with Cycle and the City. This fun bike trip starts and ends at a hidden and genuine Dutch cafe in the city centre and is full of surprises. Funny stories, a cup of real Hague coffee, a meal and booze are all included. For groups of eight people or more.

5 exceptional places to
EXPLORE NATURE

---

466 PIER HEADS OF SCHEVENINGEN

Scheveningen –
Harbour ⑤

The pier heads attract fishermen and birdwatchers. Mackerel, sea bass, sole can be caught here, while wading birds, oystercatchers, grey plovers, and sometimes even seals can be spotted. The southern 'green' pier head is the longest of the two and provides the most scenic views.

467 DE ZANDMOTOR / THE SAND MOTOR

Suburbs South ⑨
dezandmotor.nl

This peninsula near Kijkduin was created by man in 2011 to protect the vulnerable Dutch coast. A large amount of sand was dumped in front of the coastline. Scientists carefully monitor how the Sand Motor develops and research whether this innovative method for coastal protection will work.

468 MEIJENDEL

AT: DE TAPUIT
(VISITOR CENTRE)
Meijendelse-
weg 40-42
Wassenaar –
Suburbs North ⑥
+31 (0)88 347 48 49
dunea.nl

When hiking or cycling in this gorgeous reserve between Scheveningen and Wassenaar, it's hard to believe that the city is just a stone's throw away. Dunes, lakes, forests and the sea make this park the perfect place to escape the hustle and bustle. The drinking water company Dunea provides several hiking and cycling routes.

469 WESTDUINPARK

Segbroek and
Loosduinen ⑨
westduinpark.nl

This nature reserve proves once more
how green The Hague is! You're close to
the city, but, surrounded by nature and
the sea, it feels like you are on vacation.
Westduinpark has a diverse landscape
with high dune tops, open white dune
valleys, forests and shrubs. To preserve
this variety, a herd of Scottish Highland
cows graze here.

470 SOLLEVELD & HYACINTH FOREST OCKENBURGH

PARK AT:
Monsterseweg 4
Loosduinen ⑨
dunea.nl
zuidhollands
landschap.nl

Peaceful and hidden. The vulnerable old
dune landscape of Solleveld, close to
Kijkduin, can only be explored with
a passe-partout, available at the drinking
water company Dunea. Adjacent to this
unique nature reserve, at country estate
Ockenburgh, you'll find the Hyacinth
Forest which is open to public. In spring
you will be dazzled by the scent and
colour of the blue hyacinths.

466 **PIER HEADS OF SCHEVENINGEN**

5 interesting ways to explore
THE WESTLAND

471 GRAPE NURSERY NIEUW TUINZIGHT

**Zwethkade Zuid 45
Den Hoorn –
Suburbs South ⑨
+31 (0)174 292 911**
druivenkwekerij.nl

The biodynamic grapes of Nieuw Tuinzight in the Westland, the 'backyard of The Hague', are juicy, tasty and super natural. The owners, Arnold and Hilde Jansen, grow several (exclusive) varieties. Bring a visit to their little shop when the grape-harvest season is around and do not miss the beautiful old grape greenhouse from 1925 near the entrance.

471 GRAPE NURSERY NIEUW TUINZIGHT

472 SONNEHOECK

Hollewatering 26
Kwintsheul –
Suburbs South ⑨
+31 (0)6 53 31 81 21
sonnehoeck.nl

This family-run grape nursery with eight grape greenhouses dates back to the 18th century, which makes Sonnehoeck one of the oldest and best-preserved grape nurseries. It's a national monument and can be visited freely on Heritage Days. Or you can book a guided tour.

473 BIKE RENTAL WESTLAND / DE PLUKTUIN

Hovenierstraat 9
Naaldwijk –
Suburbs South ⑨
+31 (0)6 22 90 55 07
fietsverhuurwestland.nl
depluktuin.nl

Rent a bike at this rental and pick up a bike route at the close-by tea garden De Pluktuin. Both are in the heart of the Westland, also known as the Glass City, because of all the greenhouses where fruits and vegetables are cultivated. This area with small villages and greenhouses is great to explore by bike.

474 KAYAK AND CANOE RENTAL PAVILION DE ZWETH

Zwet 1
Kwintsheul –
Suburbs South ⑨
+31 (0)174 290 125
dezweth.nl

Waving reeds, scenic polders with grazing cows, meadow birds. The waterways of the Westland and the adjacent Midden-Delfland are great for kayaking, canoeing and exploring nature. The owners of this small theme park offer diverse routes with various lengths through this green lung of the Randstad.

475 PLUKKERIJ FRAMBLIJ

Zwartendijk 11
Monster –
Suburbs South ⑨
+31 (0)6 12 03 15 22
plukkerijframblij.nl

Organic raspberries, strawberries, cherries, blueberries, blackberries, and more. At this nursery you can pick your own fruit in summer. Have a tea or coffee with a slice of homemade fruit pie in the garden afterwards, while the kids enjoy themselves in the playground or with the petting animals.

5 great places to
RELAX and UNWIND

────────────

476 PAKJIRA ORIGINAL THAI MASSAGE

Thomsonlaan 90-A
Segbroek ⑧
+31 (0)70 744 84 96
pakjirathai.nl

There is no better way to relax after a long, busy week than with a good massage. At this small Thai massage salon professional massage therapists from Thailand and the Philippines offer many different treatments: from a traditional Thai massage to a healing Philippine Hilot massage. Manicure and pedicure treatments are also available.

477 WELEDA CITY SPA

Aert van der
Goesstraat 27
Scheveningen –
Statenkwartier ③
+31 (0)70 219 50 79
cityspa.weleda.nl

The well-known organic beauty brand recently opened a relaxing City Spa in the Statenkwartier. The treatments are holistic in approach, which means that the massage therapist focusses on your overall well-being. A treatment reduces stress and muscle tension and encourages better circulation. And who doesn't want that?

478 BABASSU

Dagelijkse Groen-
markt 30
Old Centre ①
+31 (0)70 360 89 65
babassu.nl

A beauty shop and a spa! On the ground floor, Babassu sells products that you will not easily find elsewhere. Unique brands like the 100% natural products by Tata Harper or the exclusive colognes and products by Santa Maria Novella. Upstairs, in the spa, you can relax and recharge during one of the many beauty treatments. Booking is essential.

479 FLOATING AT HEALTH LAB DE PIER

Strandweg 152
Scheveningen –
Beach ⑤
+31 (0)70 406 25 28
healthlabdepier.nl

Ever wanted to experience zero gravity? Go floating. Float therapy allows you to lie back while floating weightlessly in salt water. It is said to elevate your mood, increase energy levels, alleviate pain and stress, and help you reach deeper levels of relaxation. The unique location of this wellness centre at the Pier of Scheveningen makes this treatment extra special.

480 CAESAR FITNESS + SPA RESORT

Mauritskade 10
Willemspark ④
+31 (0)70 820 99 10
caesar-denhaag.nl

Inside this luxurious health club and spa, you can find a beautiful reconstruction of the oldest indoor swimming pool of the Netherlands. The pool was built in 1883, but during the recent renovation of the building it turned out to be impossible to fully restore the derelict pool. The original cast iron pillars and constructions are still present, though. For members only.

The 5 most inspiring
THINGS TO LEARN

481 WINEMAKING

AT: HAAGSE
STADSWIJNGAARD
Waldorperstraat 555
Laak ⑨
haagsestads
wijngaard.nl

Dutch wine? Yes, it's possible! In 2013, behind train station Hollands Spoor, wine aficionado Tycho Vermeulen created an urban vineyard where you can 'rent' vines. At the end of the season you harvest the grapes together with other renters and turn the grapes into wine.

482 BEEKEEPING

AT: IMKERS VERENIGING
DEN HAAG
Leidsestraatweg 51
Haagse Hout ⑥
+31 (0)71 561 44 37
imkersdenhaag.nl

At this beekeeper society you'll learn everything about the interesting lives of bees and how to become a beekeeper yourself. The course is immensely popular so be prepared for a waiting list. Every first Sunday of the month, the beautiful bee garden of the society is open to the public.

483 HORSE RIDING

AT: 'S-GRAVENHAAGSCHE
STADSRIJSCHOOL
Kazernestraat 50
Voorhout ②
+31 (0)70 363 25 20
stadsrijschool.com

This small riding school, founded by King Lodewijk Napoleon at the beginning of the 19th century, is the oldest non-military school in the Netherlands. Situated in a historic monumental building just behind Lange Voorhout, it's a hidden gem. The school organises outside rides to the beach, dunes and forest.

484 STAND UP PADDLE BOARDING
AT: SUPLES DEN HAAG
Jaap Edenweg 10
Loosduinen ⑨
+31 (0)6 39 11 56 65
suplesdenhaag.nl

The southern part of The Hague, with its quiet waterways and beautiful nature, is ideal for Stand Up Paddle boarding (SUP). Job Keukens of Suples will teach you the basics, the techniques and the safety rules. For the more advanced he also organises tours through The Hague. Great exercise for body and mind!

485 SALSA
AT: LA BODEGUITA
Oude Molstraat 32-D
Hofkwartier ②
+31 (0)70 800 77 12
labodeguita.nl

Salsa never goes out of style! You can learn this energetic dance or improve your technique at La Bodeguita, a popular Latin-dance school in the historic city centre. Professional teachers will teach you the steps and rhythm. On Friday nights, the school turns into a lively salsa club where you can put your dance skills into practice.

481 WINEMAKING

Op deze plek
bevond zich tussen
circa 1500 en 1650
's lands eerste
tennisbaan
"de Caetsbaan
van de Prinsen
van Oranje"

Aangeboden door de Oranje Tennis Club
12 juni 1999

FIRST DUTCH TENNIS COURT

15 RANDOM FACTS

The 5 best **LOCAL INITIATIVES** ——————— 254

5 remarkable and unusual **URBAN DETAILS** —— 256

5 The Hague **EVENTS** not to be missed ——————— 258

The 5 best
LOCAL INITIATIVES

486 LEKKERNASSÛH

Witte de With-
straat 127
Zeehelden-
kwartier ③ ⑧
+31 (0)6 43 87 18 91
lekkernassuh.org

Want to do something good for the
planet? Subscribe to Lekkernassûh (The
Hague slang for 'good nosh'). Once a week
you can pick up organic, local, seasonal
vegetables, fruits, cheese and more for
a very reasonable price at a non-profit
market. The market is run by volunteers.
No packaging, so bring your own bag.

487 VRIENDEN VAN DEN HAAG / FRIENDS OF THE HAGUE

*vriendenvan
denhaag.nl*

This society was founded in 1973 when
the Kurhaus was at risk of being destroyed.
Several residents saved it from demolition:
'Friends of The Hague' was born. Until
today, the society is committed to ensure
that the city retains its characteristics.
Members are regularly invited on
excursions to interesting 'hidden secrets'
of The Hague. In Dutch only.

488 I'M BINCK

Laak
imbinck.nl

For many years, the Binckhorst area was a somewhat nondescript industrial zone. But not anymore: designers, architects, artists, entrepreneurs and residents are settling here. I'M BINCK was set up to make this area more visible and liveable. This platform organises and promotes many activities that contribute to the development of the area, like festivals and tours.

489 HAAGSE HUISKAMER / THE HAGUE LIVING ROOM

+31 (0)70 763 14 98
haagsehuiskamer.nl
justiceandpeace.nl/
initiatives

The integration of refugees into The Hague society doesn't happen all by itself. The platform Haagse Huiskamer brings people and organisations together to create a city in which new and old residents can feel at home. Anyone who wants to contribute to a more resilient The Hague can join.

490 DUURZAAM DEN HAAG / SUSTAINABLE THE HAGUE

Riviervismarkt 5
Old Centre ①
+31 (0)70 364 30 70
duurzaamdenhaag.nl

A green city is a city with a future! The mission of this independent foundation is to encourage residents and entrepreneurs to make the neighbourhoods of The Hague more sustainable. If you wonder how to contribute to a more sustainable The Hague yourself, visit one of the service points in town (check the website).

5 remarkable and unusual
URBAN DETAILS

491 UNDERGROUND EXPOSITIONS: DE AFFICHE GALERIJ

Spui (tram tunnel)
Old Centre ①

In the sober tram tunnel under the Spui, designed by Rem Koolhaas, The Hague Municipal Archives organises four to six free exhibitions a year, with more than 60 remarkable advertising posters on display. The posters are mostly drawn from the Municipal Archives' own collection, often designed by artists.

492 'SECRET' ENTRANCE TO THE PALACE GARDEN

Molenstraat 27-H
Hofkwartier ②

Rumour has it that this 'secret' entrance to the lush Palace Garden behind Noordeinde Palace was once used by an adventurous prince to leave or enter the palace unnoticed. Nowadays, this entrance is open to the public. Just walk to the end of Molenstraat (past the old gate) and ring the bell at number 27-H.

493 FIRST DUTCH TENNIS COURT

AT: THE BINNENHOF
Voorhout ②

It is hard to believe that tennis was once played at the Binnenhof. But yes, near 'the Little Tower', you will find a commemorative stone with the inscription: "At this spot between 1500 and 1650 there was the country's first tennis court 'the Caetsbaan of the Princes of Orange'".

494 ATOMIC BOMB SHELTERS

Schedelhoekshaven
(underneath Leiden
University-Campus
The Hague)
Uilebomen ②
+31 (0)70 747 01 02

These remarkable underground remnants of The Cold War are located in the vicinity of administrative centres of the central government. The Hague counts fifteen of these ingenious constructions designed to shelter ministers and top officials in case of a nuclear attack. With room for 200 people, the shelter under the former Ministry of the Interior is the largest. It can only be visited under guidance.

495 FILMS SHOT IN THE HAGUE

The Hague, with its historical centre, majestic villas, modern architecture, sandy beaches, dunes and parks, has some unique film locations to offer. Scenes of many Dutch and several international movies were shot here, like Steven Soderbergh's *Ocean's Twelve* in the Atrium of the City Hall, and Paul Verhoeven's *Black Book* (Zwartboek).

491 UNDERGROUND EXPOSITIONS: DE AFFICHE GALERIJ

5 The Hague **E V E N T S**
not to be missed

---

496 **NEW YEAR'S DIVE**
Scheveningen –
Beach
*unox.nl/
nieuwjaarsduik*

With 10.000 participants, Scheveningen hosts the largest of around 60 new year's dives held in the Netherlands. Earn a woollen hat in the national colours and a tin of traditional Dutch pea soup by jumping into the bitter cold North Sea after a night of celebrating the new year.

497 **JAZZ IN DE GRACHT**
AT: VARIOUS LOCATIONS
Voorhout
Hofkwartier
Chinatown
jazzindegracht.nl

To the dismay of jazz-loving The Hague, the annual North Sea Jazz festival changed its venue to Rotterdam. However, The Hague isn't done with jazz just yet: many (new) initiatives keep the jazz scene alive. During three days in August, for example, the city's canals are crowded with flatboats carrying jazz bands. Enjoy the free concerts while sipping a drink in the late summer sun.

498 PRINSJESDAG (PRINCE'S DAY)

AT: NOORDEINDE PALACE, LANGE VOORHOUT, BINNENHOF

Voorhout
Hofkwartier

Catch a glimpse of the King and Queen riding the Golden Coach accompanied by a military escort of honour on their way from Noordeinde Palace to the Binnenhof (Inner Court) before addressing the King's speech to the Parliament. Spot female members of Parliament wearing designer hats and male members wearing tailcoats. Every third Tuesday of September on the occasion of the opening of the Parliamentary year.

499 KONINGSNACHT & KONINGSKERMIS

AT: VARIOUS LOCATIONS & MALIEVELD

thelifeilive.nl
kermisdenhaag.nl

Where else to celebrate the King's birthday than in the city known as the royal Residence? Both on the eve of his birthday and on April 27, the free two-day *The Life I Live* popular music festival puts many bands on stages around the city centre. During two weeks leading up to King's Day, a large fair for the young and old is held on the Malieveld.

500 VLAGGETJESDAG / FLAG DAY SCHEVENINGEN

AT: SCHEVENINGEN HARBOUR

Scheveningen –
Harbour
vlaggetjesdag.com

The largest herring party of the world! Around the time the first 'new herring' of the season is brought ashore, Scheveningen celebrates 'Flag Day'. The whole village and the boats in the harbour are dressed up with flags. Fishermen's choirs sing seamen songs, children play old Dutch games, traditional arts and crafts are on display, and – obviously – herring is everywhere.

INDEX

1646 Experimental
    Art Space   196
American Book Center 127
Abdijkerk   174
About Flowers   134
Achtung! Baby   215
Alexanderhoeve
    Den Haag   91
Algemene Begraafplaats
    Kerkhoflaan   177
Alice in Wonderland   212
Aloha   131
Amare   142
Amazing Oriental
    Ypenburg   101
Antique and
    Book Market   89
Appel & Ei   119
Arendsdorp & Park
    Oostduin   164
Art & Casey   121
Atlantikwall Bike
    Tour   242
Atlantikwall Museum
    Scheveningen   193
Au petit pont   135
Avonturia
    de Vogelkelder   219
Baardman   28
Babassu   249
Bacán B&B   225
Bakkerij Maxima   55
Baladi Manouche   54
Bartine   27
Beeld en Geluid
    Den Haag   217
Bendorff   123
Bennies Fifties   108
Berry Rutjes   133

Bike rental Westland
    / De Pluktuin   247
Bistro Mer   40
Bleyenberg   80
Blossom   71
BLOW! Kitesurfing
    School   237
Boat trips   234
Bonbon-Atelier
    Westerbeek   98
Bookstor   66
BOON   97
Boots by M   124
Boulangerie Michel   94
Bouzy, Wine & Food   78
Branoul   194
BRICKS 'Hooch & Brew' 80
Buddha Bowl   30
Burgemeester
    de Monchyplein   164
Burger Bar   54
Bøg   33
CaDance Festival   202
Caesar Fitness
    + Spa Resort   249
Café Aimée   51
Café Constant   50
Café De Kleine Witte   82
Café de la Gare   75
Café de Oude Mol   83
Café de Sien   83
Café Franklin   50
Canals   180-181
Capriole Café   65
Carlton Ambassador   230
Casa Capello   49
Catshuis   155
Central Library   69
Chambers of Wonder 217

Club Vers   26
Coast Fish   41
Coffee Works   68
Contemporary
    architecture   141
Couqou   110
Cove Centrum   230
Crossing Border
    Festival   198
Crunch   24
Curry & Cocos   45
Cycle and the City   243
Cycle Tour Castle
    Duivenvoorde   242
Dalton School   140
Dayang   42
DCR   196
De Bonte Koe   99
De Boomhuttenclub   221
De Dutch Don't
    Dance Division   203
De filosoof   102
De Galerie Den Haag 128
De Haagse Bijenkorf   140
De Haagse Markt   88
De Huishoudwinkel   110
De Jutterskeet   219
De Kade   78
De Kikkerkoning   212
De Kornoelje   161
De Kwartel   53
De Nieuwe Regentes   195
De Overkant   26
De Paas   76
De Parade Den Haag   199
De Pier   152
De Pier, Suites
    & Cabins   226
De Rode Loper   125

De Staat	53	
De Sushimeisjes	44	
De Tapperij	50	
De Vries Van Stockum	127	
De Waterkant	221	
De Zandmotor	244	
Deja Vintage	108	
Diligentia & PePijn	194	
Domus Spinozana	154	
Douwes	126	
Drogisterij van der Gaag	104	
DS Patisserie	94	
Dudok	68	
Dürst Britt & Mayhew	129	
Edwin Pelser	112	
Elpidio	93	
Elvis & Otis	214	
Embassy Festival	198	
Emma's Hof	161	
Escher in The Palace	217	
Espresso Perfetto	97	
ETTEMADIS	122	
Europol	157	
Evy's	119	
Fat Kee	46	
Filmhuis Den Haag	197	
Filtro	65	
Filya Indoor Garden	134	
Fleur's	67	
Floating at Health Lab De Pier	249	
Florencia	58	
FOAM	31	
Free Beer Co.	105	
Full Moon City	46	
Galerie Guthschmidt	117	
Galerie Ramakers	129	
Gallery Prince William V	189	
Garden behind the Kunstmuseum	162	
Gember	72	
Glaswerk	35	
Goedman art supplies	105	
Gransjean	93	

Grape nursery Nieuw Tuinzight	246	
Grapes & Olives	77	
Greens	74	
Haagse Boomtoppers	218	
Haagse Kunstkring	128	
Haagse Strandhuisjes	226	
Hagedis	32	
Handelingenkamer	182	
Haringkar Harteveld	56	
Haringkraam Buitenhof	57	
Hart Beach Surf School	236	
Haver	28	
Heden	128	
Heilige Antonius Abtkerk	144	
Heilige Geest Hofje	168	
Het Apenbos	211	
Het Appeltaartgevoel	115	
Het Haags Wijnhuis	103	
Het Haringhuisje	57	
Het IJskabinet	58	
Het Puntje	53	
Hidden streets	171	
High tea boat	71	
Hofje van Nieuwkoop	169	
Hof van Wouw	169	
Holland Dance Festival	202	
Hoppzak	75	
Hop & Stork	98	
Hostel The Hague	229	
Hotel des Indes	71	
Hotel Indigo	231	
Hotel Pistache	225	
House of Hats	105	
House of Tribes	69	
Hout Sage Speelgoed	213	
HUG THE TEA	70	
Huis de Zeemeeuw	145	
Huis ten Bosch Palace	151	
Huis van Lorrie	145	
HUmmUS	32	
Huppel the Pub	82	
Huygens' Hofwijck	155	
Huykman & Duyvestein	125	

Ibis Styles City Centre	231	
Ilka Vintage	118	
India Gate	100	
Indisch Monument	166	
Inproc	96	
International Criminal Court	156	
Jan van Goyen House	155	
Japanese garden	162	
Jazz in de gracht	258	
Jewish Cemetery	175	
Jorplace Beach Hostel	228	
Juni Café	30	
JUST	121	
Kaafi	64	
Kaasspeciaalzaak Ed Boele	90	
Kali Tengah	97	
Kalkman	91	
Kasteel de Wittenburg	227	
Kayak and canoe rental Pavilion de Zweth	247	
Keraton Damai	43	
Kinderboekenmuseum	216	
King Falafel	54	
KingKool	228	
Kloosterkerk	151	
KM21 & Fotomuseum Den Haag	186	
Kneuterdijk Palace	150	
Kompaan Craft Beer Bar	75	
Koningsnacht & Koningskermis	259	
Kooman's Poppentheater	218	
Korzo	195	
Korzo India Dance Festival	203	
Kroon Kaashandel	90	
Kunstmuseum Den Haag / The Hague Art Museum	188	
Kurhaus with high tea	240	
La Paulowna	225	
La Rana	74	

La Sorentina	49	Moofer's Salon	132	Paagman	126
La Venezia	58	Mr. Bap	44	Paard	200
Laan van		Murphy's Law	201	Pakjira Original	
Meerdervoort	145	Museon	216	Thai Massage	248
Lapsang	77	Museum Beelden aan		Paleistuin	160
Lasas & Loekov	111	Zee / Sculptures		Palmette	74
Laurie Hermeler	117	by the Sea	186	Panorama Mesdag	188
Le Café	77	Museum Bike Tour by		Papaverhof	138
Le Marie Marché	88	Haagsche Stadsfiets	243	Parimar boeken	127
Le Petit Quartier	28	Museum Bredius	190	Park Clingendael	159
Lekker Brood	94	Museum de Gevangen-		Park Sorghvliet	163
Lekkernassûh	254	poort / Prison Gate		Pastanini	49
Lente Thee en		Museum	190	Pastis	38
Chocolade	97	Museum Meermanno	193	Pâtisserie Chocolaterie	
Liesbeth Busman	116	Museum Voorlinden	187	Jarreau	99
Literatuurmuseum /		Museum Voorlinden		Peace Palace	156
Museum		Library	183	Peace Palace Library	182
of Literature	193	Muziekcafé De Paap	201	Pepita d'Oro	117
Little Green Shop	135	Nationaal Archief	183	Peppermint	24
Little V	37	Nationaal Monument		Perron X Coffee	
littleYOU	215	Oranjehotel	166	Roasters	68
Lokaal Duinoord	82	Naturel	53	Philippe Galerne	95
Lola Bikes and Coffee	66	NDT (Nederlands		Pier heads of	
Lookout at Vogelwijk	152	Dans Theater)	203	Scheveningen	244
Lorelei	51	New Year's Dive	258	Piet Artisans of Flavour	59
Louis Couperus	154, 179	NicoNico	125	Pistache Café	29
Louwman Museum	192	Nirwanaflat	138	Planet Jump	211
Luciano	59	Noordeinde	144	Plenty	31
Madestein		Noordeinde Palace	151	Pluk! Den Haag	221
Recreational Park	238	Noordzee Boardstore	130	Plukkerij Framblij	247
Mandarin Palace	47	Nudist beaches	239	Pluk & Paloma	215
Manus Skateshop	131	Nutstuin	162	Podium	
Marakesh	100	Ohana Poké and More	29	De Nieuwe Kamer	200
Maranathakerk	174	Oh Dear	117	Pompernikkel	28
Marius		Old-Catholic Clandestine		Pompke	67
Jouw Wijnvriend!	103	Church	173	Portfolio	33
MAS	112	Old Pine Shop	106	Poush.	109
Matruschka	213	Oma Toos	220	PR8T1G	110
Mauritshuis	189	Omniversum	218	Present Living	108
Meermanno		Oni	45	Prinsjesdag	
Miniature Library	183	Oogst	34	(Prince's Day)	259
Meijendel	244	OPCW	157	Prodemos	241
Meza	93	Op z'n kop	71	Proefhuys	91
Michael Barnaart	132	Organic Market	88	Pulchri Studio	197
Modern public art	206	Oud Eik en Duinen	175	QUERU Cantina	
Monkeybos	211	Own & Club	121	Mexicana	36

Rabbijn Maarsenplein 165
Radar Cafe by Popradar 200
Ramen Ohashi 45
Reinhard Frans 124
Residenz
    Stadslogement 224
Restaurant 6&24 34
Restaurant CRU 38
Restaurant ñ 36
RN Productos Latinos 101
Rood Met Witte Stippen 212
Room 72
Royal Christmas Fair 89
Royal Stables 151
Royal Waiting Room 241
Russian Church 173
Rusthof 168
Sam Sam 26
Saplab Slowjuice 29
Scheveningse Bosjes 159
Sculpture Garden
    Clingenbosch 240
Seafood BAR Vigo 41
Secrid 133
Shaka 131
Sickboards 131
Simonis aan de Haven 57
Single Estate Coffee
    Roasters – De Bar 64
Sint Hubertuspark 163
Skatepark De Kuil &
    Zandspeeltuin 210
Skatepark Sweatshop 210
Slapen op De Boot /
    Sleeping on
    The Boat 226
Solleveld & Hyacinth
    Forest Ockenburgh 245
Sonnehoeck 247
SPOOKY & SUE 118
Sprinkel + Hop 106
Stadsvilla Mozaic 225
Staybridge Suites 230
Stijlbandiet 109
Stokstaart 215
Store Du Nord 122

St. Petrus Banden 177
Strandpaviljoen Zuid 52
Street art and murals 204
Stroom Den Haag 197
Studio Mrs. Rosehip 133
Studio van 't Wout 112
Sunny Court 164
Surinaamse Markt 100
Suzie Q 37
't Hooftshofje 169
Tapisco 38
Tartine 88
Teleport Hotel 229
Ter Navolging 177
That's Amore 49
The Chocolate-shop 99
The Five Points 79
The Flower Kitchen 134
The Garden House 227
The Hague Beach
    Stadium 236
The Hague Bike Tours 243
The Hague Public
    Transport Museum 192
The Hague's Finest 114
The Hague statues 178
The Hague Tower of
    the Grote Kerk 153
The Harbour Club 153
The Historical Museum
    of The Hague 190
The International
    Residual Mechanism
    for Criminal
    Tribunals 157
The Shore 237
The Student Hotel 229
Theater aan het Spui 195
Tigershark 64
Toko Bali Mandira 42
Toko Menteng 42
Toko Sawa 43
Tommy's & Zuurveen 34
Tong Tong Fair 199
Toren van Oud 140
Traiteur Le Gône 93

Ultramarijn 80
Uptown 123
Van Kinsbergen 76
VanPeet 120
VaVoom Tiki Room 79
Vegan Pizza Bar 31
Vers uit de Gers 92
Villa Ockenburg –
    De Kas 220
Villa Windekind 167
Vincenzo's 48
Vino Vero 102
Visafslag Scheveningen
    / fish auction 241
Vishandel de Lange 57
Vlaggetjesdag / Flag Day
    Scheveningen 259
Vlietland 239
Vlietland 152
Vuurtoren 152
Waalsdorpervlakte 165
WAAR 115
Walter Benedict 35
Warung Mini 55
Wassenaarse Slag 238
Waterproef 41
Watt Design 111
WAUW 114
Weleda City Spa 248
Wempe & Wempe 105
Westbroekpark 158
Westduinpark 245
White 123
Wiener Konditorei 67
Wijnhandel Kooper 103
Willibrordus House 174
Winston & Wei Wei 47
Winternachten 199
WNKL 114
Wox 40
WWen 121
Yoga on the beach 237
Zebedeüs 36
Zheng 46
Zuiderpark 158
ZUSJES vintage boetiek 118
Zwembad De Put 238

COLOPHON

EDITING, COMPOSING *and* PHOTOGRAPHY — Tal Maes
talmaes.com — kitchentablefood.com
GRAPHIC DESIGN — Joke Gossé and doublebill.design
COVER IMAGE — Kunstmuseum Den Haag (secret 345)

The addresses in this book have been selected after thorough independent research by the author, in collaboration with Luster Publishing. The selection is solely based on personal evaluation of the business by the author. Nothing in this book was published in exchange for payment or benefits of any kind.

D/2022/12.005/25
ISBN 978 94 6058 3292
NUR 511, 510

© 2019 Luster, Antwerp
Third edition, September 2022 — Second reprint, September 2022
lusterpublishing.com — THE500HIDDENSECRETS.COM
info@lusterpublishing.com